Previously Published Poems

"The Cricket Sings My Song" – published in <u>Poetry '74</u>, 1974, *Poetry Brokers*

"Take the Rainbow for a Dime" – published in <u>Harvest</u>, 1975, *Harvest Publishers*

"Life of the Wind" – published in <u>The Bicentennial Voice</u>, 1976, *The Sterling Press*

"Dark Moods" – published in <u>Quiet Thoughts</u>, 1979, *Poetry Press*

A Collection of Poetry

Seasons of the Heart

YOLANDA G. GUERRA

authorHOUSE®

AuthorHouse™
1663 Liberty Drive
Bloomington, IN 47403
www.authorhouse.com
Phone: 1 (800) 839-8640

Compiled by Sylvia Y. Stankewich
Edited by Janet W. Butler

Published by AuthorHouse 03/15/2017

ISBN: 978-1-5246-7555-4 (sc)
ISBN: 978-1-5246-7554-7 (hc)
ISBN: 978-1-5246-7553-0 (e)

Library of Congress Control Number: 2017903698

Print information available on the last page.

Ah, when to the heart of man was it ever less than a treason to go with the drift of things to yield with a grace to reason and bow and accept at the end of a love or a season.

—Robert Frost

Be Strong

"Say not the days are evil.
Who's to blame? And fold the hands and say,
oh, shame!
Stand up! Speak out, and bravely,
in God's name, be strong!"

— Yolanda G. Guerra

Contents

Acknowledgments

I wish to express my sincere thanks to Janet W. Butler for her outstanding editorial skills and guidance in the development of this book.

I also want to thank my family for their encouragement and assistance while I embarked on this project.

And most of all, I thank my late mother and the author, Yolanda G. Guerra, for her gift of over half a century's work of poetry that she left to myself and my brothers to treasure. May her memory never fade.

Sylvia Y. Stankewich
(daughter of the author)

Introduction

Yolanda Grace Guerra never claimed to be a professional writer; perhaps that was why, over a period of time in which she wrote these deeply personal reflections on life, love, and a myriad of other emotions, she consistently declined to submit the major part of her work for publication. Only four of the poems here — indicated on the Previously Published Poems page — ever actually were released for public view. The rest, Guerra kept in her private collection, until she passed away. Years prior to Guerra's passing, her daughter had made a solemn promise to her mother that she would publish Guerra's poems after her death to not only honor her mother's memory but to also give others a chance to appreciate her gift of writing poetry. This book, SEASONS OF THE HEART, has been assembled now, as a loving tribute from Guerra's family.

We have divided these poems into thematic sections and ordered them by year to give the reader a sense of the ebb and flow of this woman's poetry, as it paralleled the ebb and flow of life events. Like many of us, Guerra had more than her share of difficulties; unlike many of us, she put down on paper how those difficulties affected her, the reactions they drew from her and the conclusions (for good or ill) to which they brought her. From the simple joys of raising children to the torment of lost love, Guerra lets the reader glimpse life through a very particular lens. You will see here a kaleidoscope of images from the somber grays of a winter sky to verdant bursts of spring, and from delicate tracery on a butterfly to silvery iridescence of rain...seen through the eyes of a soul equally able to burst forth in joyful song or tears of despair.

And it's no accident that so much of Guerra's expressiveness is spelled out in terms of natural imagery: her favorite place in all the world was the outdoors. When she was happy, it became her dance floor; when she mourned, it wrapped its timeless arms around her and soothed her pain. The small country towns of south Texas, the quiet, desolate ranch, rambling dusty roads, gardens and clear, running creeks — these were the places she understood and cherished most of all. It's not surprising, therefore, that at the end of her life she speaks of going back to "...*my green trees, my fields, my country roads…"* Surrounded by the great outdoors, she perseveres through her journey despite the trials and upheavals inherent in a life too often hemmed-on and restricted.

Here, on these pages, that life could be freed; here, on these pages, it is explored and expressed. Here, on these pages, a reader may find a mirror — and a deeper understanding — that in the end, we're more alike than different in how what we see, touch, taste, smell, and hear affects and shapes us all. Here, on these pages, we can read, and contemplate, how life touches us all.

We, her children, are honored to share SEASONS OF THE HEART with you. May it touch your life, no matter the season in which you may find yourself.

Greeting

Welcome to this journal of a life…a kaleidoscope of moments, emotions, and introspections over half a century.

A life lived. A life savored. A life celebrated!

Live for Today (1978)

I think that I should think—
oh life, as life sees me—
that life be kind to me today.

Tomorrow who knows what will bring;
that I go out and dance among the fireflies
with arms outstretched to reach the sky;
for time just might catch up with me.

Live now! Dance a ballet among the silver raindrops—
who knows? The rain might never come again.

Family

We begin our journeys on this earth placed into
families. They form us. They shape us. They instill in
us things that, for good or for ill, last a lifetime.

They are the places from which we take our first steps, and
the places where we encourage first steps in others.

They are the beginning.

My Father (1964)

Each new day that comes will bring the face of yesterday—
those dear old faces that were young
will look at me with faded eyes.
Their trembling hands will then hold mine.

No more will I see that tall, lean man.
Yes, he—it was my father that used to be.
I wake up each day to find a gray old man—
who now stumbles in the dark as he thinks of yesterday.

A man I never saw before hold back because of fear—
a man who used to stand so tall,
shedding not a tear while others were in sight.

I do not know this man; my father didn't walk bent low!
He used to stand so tall, while he worked his fingers
to the bone.
He cared for us, he must have once—
that man there, he cannot be my father!

Little Child (1968)

(For Gary)

Little child, your face is love,
your hair is sunshine, your eyes the sky!
Those little hands tell me of dependence
on Mom and Dad for loving guidance.
Yet, little one, sky, love, and sunshine
is what you've given
your mom and dad by being ours.

My Dad (1969)

He was a lonely man, yes, he;
he had a family, and he had me.
He was alone now in his old age,
alone in a room, away from me.

We were not far, yet didn't find time
to fill his room with you and me.
He was alone, yet in the end
he found a home with God, away from you and me.

He left me and he left you; see, he left with God—
you and I ran out of time.

The Wooden Horse (1973)

(Dedicated to my three children)

The wooden horse my child once played with
sits now alone out on the porch.
Rider-less and lonely, colorless and dusty,
the once-proud owner now long gone.

The shouts of glee from my young boy
still echo throughout the house.
And that wooden horse he played with so
is lonely now the child is gone.

Classroom Nuisance (1973)

(For my two sons)

Teacher, teacher, lift a hand,
but only to try and understand.
I know my voice is so high-pitched
and so low when you ask me to speak.
I also stutter when I read,
and two plus two is three to me.
I try, I try, I really do,
but being nine must be the reason
I daydream when I should be studying religion.
I squirm, I talk, I make such noise;
my nine-year ways they can't accept;
I try to sit so sweet and still
but being boy makes my feet kick,
my tongue to move—I can't sit still.
Teacher, teacher, maybe when I'm ten,
I'll win a prize for being a perfect gentleman.
I try to sit so sweet and still
while at my desk to please you still.
But being nine and being boy
makes my feet kick,
and my tongue move—
I try, I do, to sit real still,
but then, a fly comes buzzing by
and Teacher comes by and snaps at me.
I squirm, I talk, I make such noise;
my nine-year ways
they can't accept.
Oh, Teacher, Mother, Dad, and friends!
Just wait until I'm ten!
Then maybe I will sit and face teacher's desk.

Gary's Ball (1973)

At this moment, you're so big!
You're really in the major leagues.
Roll and tumble, raise some dust—
oh! You've torn your brand-new jeans.

Nine-year-old, you act so big—
you imagine yourself in the major leagues.
But then you shout, "Mom, they cheat!"
Dusty and torn, you come to me.

Batter up! You stand so tall
when, really, you are quite small.
The ball sails now across the field;
you're now flat on your back.

The Beach (1976)

On a day warm and golden,
barefoot by the sea, I play.
I build sand castles
while the sea shells show their colors.

My little sister thinks she sees a pirate ship;
it turns out to be a tugboat!
My little brother says he found a spider—
I laugh; it's a baby crab!

Everything about the sea, I love—
the wind, it keeps on touching me;
the sand is warm under me;
the sky and seagulls reach for me.

Bonnie's Horse (1979)

Bonnie, she's my child,
and Bonnie rides a poor deaf horse.

But the horse, it hears through Bonnie,
for Bonnie has a great big heart!

Beautiful is my Bonnie!
Gentle is her heart.

The deaf horse hears her songs.
By looking in her eyes, he
understands the mirror of her soul.

I Am Their Souls (1980)

(A Mother's Song)

I am that part of them
that can't say no.
That part of them that gives all.

I am the smile they never give.
The part of them that's supposed to forgive.
I am the part of them that laughs at all.

I am the part of them when they dream
and the hand of theirs that holds, I am.
I am the part of them that keeps the nightmares from
their nights.

I am that, that which cradles them,
the same as they would cradle
a sleeping kitten or a friend.

If I am that part of them,
why are they not a part of me?
The part of me that loves and cries at
loneliness in the night?

If I am that part of them
that sings and cries at night,
what makes me sad to look at them?

(Cont'd next page)

I Am Their Souls, *cont'd*

I am the part that takes their pain;
I am their part that lies awake—
the part that knows their age!

I am them when, just a child,
their fevered dreams led them to cry.
I am their souls when love they want!

So, what am I when I am them?
When their wrongs and loves tear me apart.
I am their souls when they cry out.

I am that part of them that lends a hand,
a hand that leads them into some fairyland.
I am the part of them that stops the pain!

I am, I am, and they now know
to call on me when nights get long.
I am their soul, and I live long!

For Gary, My Son (1984)

I would tell you stories,
and you would tell me tales.
You were full of wonder then, my boy,
and I was full of awe!
You saw the world,
and I, I saw you as if you were a doll!
We'd search out goldfish
in ponds of glass, and birds to you
were dreams you planned to catch!
And now you're leaving;
you're now of age.
A handsome young man
must search his fate.
You'll come and see me, now and then.
you'll tell me stories;
I'll tell you tales.

In My Mother's House (1994)

Unable to obtain forgiveness,
I, not wanting to forgive,
I walk the long, dark halls
of my mother's unforgiving house.

I cannot reach the end,
for I would have to drift
and just let the past be dead,
and that would be to forgive.

You almost reach forgiveness
when a ghost of childhood past
comes walking down the hallway
of my mother's angry, unforgiving house.

I cannot reach the light
as I walk my darkened heart
and house and home become two places
at the end of empty halls.

Faith

From our homes and from our mothers' arms, we reach out to the world and to whomever we can know or envision as God.

Our faith can ebb, and it can flow. It can increase, and it can decrease. It can be shattered, and put back together again.

When we come to a place where it settles us, we are at peace.

Humanity (1969)

And God bent down
      to look at us.
He bowed his head in sorrow
      to see what we'd become.

Each of us so arrogant;
      so sure we knew it all.
God cried a tear today
      and we never once looked up.

Judgment (1974)

Don't blame the tree
for the leaves that fall
or the wind for the shifting sands;
there's so much you cannot see.

Don't blame the rain
for the flower that didn't grow
or the cold for the birds that left;
there's so much you'll never know.

Don't blame a good man
for the souls he couldn't save,
but do blame ourselves for the acts
that turned to shame!

Their Ignorance (1988)

I have talked before
    about suns being beneath my feet
    and above my head.
But I am sad—no others think about that.
    They live their lives and never think
    that God is watching their every step.

How sad to think they believe my God has no control;
    they give their lives to fun and games
and disrespect is out of their mouths.
    If they would think for just one moment
    of suns beneath their feet and suns above their heads.

My Final Love (2000)

I don't feel I want to go
to dust, to ashes, or to dirt.
And God frowns down on me
when I would rather be a star.

When, instead of dust,
I'd rather be the rain that gleams on a tree.
When, instead of ashes, make of me
a statue high as all the pyramids.

So God frowns down on me
because I will not be
like all the creatures big and small,
and believe ash as my final love.

A Glimpse of Eternity (2001)

I looked into eternity today.
I lost myself in darkness;
so frightened I became;
I drew back into the light.

A voice said I was privileged
to see what others don't.
Come forward, look;
you're allowed only a moment.

I looked in, but was unable
to see and hear and keep
my balance and my mind,
so I drew back, content to stay behind.

Nostalgia

As we explore forward, we also look backward. Our families, our friends, our work, our feelings...they give us our first memories. We long for what we see as simpler, easier, better times.

Yet we also know that looking backward can remind us of things we'd thought we forgotten — and hoped to leave forgotten. Nostalgia can bring smiles, or tears. Bliss, or heartbreak.

We approach the mist of memory with a tentative step, understanding that sometimes, the mist that makes memories unclear is a mercy.

His Memory (1969)

The man who kept a Christmas tree
longer than all of us hold a memory.
The man who hoped to have someone
to share the smells and lights of it.

He kept it long, for no one came,
and his tree was dead long before the memories.
Christmas came and went,
but no one came to share it.

Autumn Leaves (1971)

I keep seeing them!
Those autumn leaves
that never cease to fall on time each year.

I used to try and catch one when I was just a child.
And when I had one in my hand, another caught my eye!

I'm now more than just a child.
And the autumn leaves still fall on time.
I concentrate now on the colors, and hold several at one time.

Reflections (1973)

I woke to memories today.
My dreams were filled
with faces of so many years ago.
In them was he who changed my life—
he whom I left because youth called.

> And now I sit and take out memories—
> an old, old picture I carry still.

As hurt now fills inside of me,
I wondered how I never knew
that it was he who was why I never loved again.
I wonder now as I see his picture
how many years it's been—

> and if he, too, remembers me
> and loves me, loves me still.

Soft Voices (1976)

I thought I heard soft voices,
but the night wind was the one
that cried.
How could I have heard soft sounds
when the dancing was so wild?

How could I hear the voice inside
of me (or even inside of you)
when the earth spun so fast
and the leaves liquefied
and drenched us with a
greenish foam?

In that darkened tavern
where we claim we go for fun,
I heard the soft sounds
of men moaning,
hurting deep inside.

So Long Ago (1978)

Soul that knows no boundaries
to the trappings of my heart.
Like a stranger on the run,
I am tired of the road.
        I am tired of your anger,
        I am tired of the words—
        empty words that have no knowledge
        of the way your heart unfolds.
Soul, you've got to let me
find the one real road I lost—
also, find a youthful laughter that was me,
so long ago.

The Day the Butterflies Disappeared (1981)

We'd gather 'round my best friend's porch.
Veins and veins climbed the walls
of lovely pink flowers that
the butterflies loved so.

Those butterflies were lonely daydreams
touching down on large and small blossoms alike.
And my and my friends' hearts would touch
each blossom same as they.

With those black and yellow butterflies, my friend
and I would touch the skies
For as we swung on the porch swing,
my friend and I, laughing, became
beautiful butterflies.

It was after we'd grown up,
after years of having lived apart,
We went back to see the butterflies.
But they were gone; insecticides, I hear,
had made all the butterflies disappear.

And my friend's and my heart flew off
with the lost black and yellow butterflies.

The Song of Change (1988)

I heard it then, the song of change.
But I was young and kept on going
the same direction.

I heard the song later; sad I was by then,
too sad to know it was the song of change,
the change I should have made
to save my soul all its pain.

The last call came: I heard the song,
I took a chance and changed it all.

Each day that I awaken, I take a chance,
but I'm changing it for all I'm worth.

There Was a Time (1988)

Too many voices rang out;
all of them too loud—
for there was a time when
flowers and trees talked,
but later, these other voices drowned them out.

A time when birds would stop and listen,
while rain fell in pastel lights
and little children knew that dreams go on,
and they could hold them in their arms.
Yes, a time when flowers and trees talked.

When we could leave our bodies
and fly and touch the stars,
and the stars would love for us to visit.
It turned out that it was children
who stopped the dreams from going on.

I Dreamt of Children (1989)

Today I saw the children play;
they seem to be of no age at all—
they were all sizes,
that I know.
Their faces showed nothing at all.

The playground had no swings or slides
yet, the children played round and round.
I couldn't see the color of their eyes;
couldn't hear their voices,
yet, I could tell them apart.

Old Memories (2012)

Last night I dreamed
of old places, old faces,
old memories.

They danced, they laughed,
they cried,
all for me in the memory.

The sand and snarled trees—
the wind with its old song
were all on stage for me to see.

A child with new patent leather shoes
and braids with ribbons blowing,
she held her hand out—to whom?

Loneliness

Is there any other human feeling so universal? We
suspect not: no matter where you are in the world,
even surrounded by crowds, you can feel alone.

Loneliness goes beyond mere solitude into longing, a specific longing
to be known deeply by at least one other person. Loneliness propels us
toward many people in our lives, in a quest for that "one" who'll truly
know us as we want to be known.

Loneliness is the soul seeking home.

Old Woman's Cry (1960)

My hands are tired with toil.
My heart, weary with grief.
My bones are nothing but aches,
My wrinkles show clear on my face.

I've got nothing to show I was young once;
I am bent over from life's beatings.
I have no one to share with;
My nights are spent turning pages.

Because I Loved (1973)

Because I loved, I gave my all.
And drained of all,
they asked for more.
My life was spent in giving.
And then one day I saw
that as I turned to look,
ALL of them were gone.

The hands I used in giving
are now old and worn.
And weary are my steps
as I turn to go up to my room.
I never get a letter—
I hardly hear the phone—
I wait so patiently
for those I gave my all!

Alone (1973)

I am alone in the midst of all confusion.
As alone as a flower that stands apart
in a field full of wildflowers.
I am alone as only silence can be
in a room full of people;
as alone as a bird that strays
from its flock.
I am alone as a baby, being born,
finds its mother gone.
I am as alone as one star shining
with the nearing dawn.
My loneliness just grows.

Searching the Valleys (1974)

I must walk down the valleys;
my heart has wearied again.
And I must search for the answers—
listen to the calls in my head.

I search the valleys in vain,
for the answers never come easy as rain.
And my youth is slipping away—
my memory picking at long-lost pain.

My spirit flies within valleys
when the heart is weary and cold,
and I alone, must bring it back,
for the rest of the world holds its own.

I Am Tired, Very Tired (1974)

Tonight, I can't sleep.
There's no warmth in the fire.
    The pounding rain mocks on;
    it keeps all other sounds quiet.
Tonight, I am very tired.
I know how the ground feels after the storm.
    Far away are the stars;
    I feel my God far away.
I don't want to think of tomorrow
or that the warmth of summer comes.
    Tonight, I don't want to think of myself;
    I don't want to think of others.
I am very, very tired—
silence is my only welcome guest.

Take Me Home (1974)

Lost, lonely, and alone—
stranger, tell me, could you take me home?
Funny, how the second loss
can be as painful as your first.
Stranger, I'm lost, lonely and alone,
please take me home!

> I need warm arms, kind words
> more than drink in front of me.
> I can be warm and loving,
> stranger; you'll never want to let
> me go.

I Was a Child (1977)

I laugh, now that conscience directs me;
before that, I never did laugh.
I carried on, and life was fine.
I was a child in a room full of toys,
taking each one apart,
then looking sadly around,
thinking to myself that there was
no one around to scold me,
and I felt sad.

My Loneliness (1978)

I mourn for him
who cannot hear my songs.
I mourn for him
who lies fruitless, eyes void,
my own body ready for his love.

I weep! And he lies there in vain.
I mourn because I've known his touch!
And now, he cannot even see my face!
I mourn, all love expired with his death.

My loneliness, it is no one else's pain!
No one sees the anguish that now drives me *mad*.
Every joy inside me has expired;
I am as fruitless as he, lying there!

Solita (1978)

(The Solitary One)

Solita, the sole one of her dreams.
The lonely one who stood there
and no one cared.
Solita, alone like the sun—the moon—
the furthest star. Solita, alone in the
       midst of it all.

Solita, give us your smile,
but no, Solita does not know how.
Solita has been alone too long.

Empty (1982)

How do I speak to anyone?
My voice has left my head.
My heart has frozen;
I cannot think ahead.

I live an empty world;
I know not love or thought.
But raise the window
and breathe the ones out there.

They cannot see me—
their eyes are dead.
I plead for mercy—
come, see my lonely self.

But loneliness is something
that no one cares to have.
The birds stand at my window
and their hearts bleed to death.

Sad Little Houses (1982)

We all live in our sad little houses.
We walk with our heads high
and our hearts low.

We sing our sad little songs
and talk like we don't owe a thing
to the world.

We live our lives like a song.
go to bed still pretending,
and wake to dried-up tears in our eyes.

Why can't we help one another?
Help fill those empty spots in our hearts
and color our sad little houses…
        every color…
                in all the world.

The Wind (1982)

My eyes looked up to see the dawn;
they looked down low and saw my heart.
It lay in pieces there in the dirt
with all the things that it had lost.

I know the wind does not tell
the sound the heart makes
as it breaks;
instead, the wind moans its tale.

Oh, I do not want to be the wind.
The wind has so many stories to tell—
that's why it's never very still,
and, oh, love doesn't live here.

I Speak but No One Hears (1983)

I talk, but no one hears,
and when they speak,
I hope to hear what I voice in my own mind.
And I end up lonely,
lonelier than the furthest star.

I see reflections in the waters.
All the faces are strangers;
they all look at me with empty eyes.
I end up needing, wanting,
and I know not what!

I sink, lower than I ever have.
I seem to be at destiny's end.
I speak and no one understands.
I lose them, and lose myself.

My Children (1988)

I was the tree that dropped the seeds
that were to give birth to three young trees.
What I did not know was that someday,
I would be left to die alone.

The trees grew strong and tall,
and I was left to watch
as they drank the moisture from the ground,
and I was left to die of thirst.

I didn't see ahead of time
that someday, they wouldn't look down
to see what was happening to me,
and that there was no way they could drop a seed
that would give life to me.

The bitter end came faster than I thought.
I shivered in the winter
and burned in the sun.
Without nourishment, the wind took me away.

My Wall (1989)

My nights are long,
the day so harsh.
And in the wall I hear a cry—
a cry that seems to come from me.

I know I've pushed them all away,
but I was gone before they came.
There was a way for them to have changed things,
but the voice in the wall they did not hear.

I now have pushed their voices into the wall
and made the wall so thick I cannot hear!
Myself, I hear often at night
and the whimpers come from deep inside.

I can't escape these long, long nights,
and yet I'm gone so far
that I can't see them anywhere,
and I let them burn in the harsh daylight.

I Am an Old House (2000)

I am an old house
with its corridors empty
and the halls all dark.

I stand there, silent,
my windows shut
because someone let me down.

I am an old house
that no one loves
and I stand finished and yet undone.

Love

When we have found that "one" who understands us, who truly knows us and accepts us...there is love. And what a joy it is to be able to give and receive love!

We love many times and many people in our lives, and it is something a human being never stops seeking. When we find it, the songs break forth in our lives and in our hearts.

When we are filled with love, we feel as if we have at last "arrived."

Do I Love Thee (1959)

Do I love thee like a gentle river?
Crystal-like and smooth?
Or do I love thee like a raging sea,
full of stormy melody?

Ride the Stars (1970)

I want to light the skies
with my dreams.
I want to go on forever
riding the stars with my dreams.

I want to share my dreams
with you, and her, and him,
and ride the stars forever.

The Gift of Quiet (1972)

You gave me quiet
as we held hands.
I'd never been so happy
as when you never said a word.

Gentle, peaceful quiet
was what I needed most;
that raging storm my life had been
subsided gently in your arms.

Quiet, peaceful quiet—
not a word we spoke;
yet gently, ever quiet,
you made me love you more.

I Became Lost (1973)

The first time you made love to me,
I cried.
The second time was heaven,
but I dug out all the flowers
from my garden.
The third time after that,
I had to have you
time and time again.
Time was lost; spring, to me, was fall
and winter became summer;
morning became evening;
night, to me, was noon.
For wanting you, I became lost.

I Think of You (1973)

To think of you, I think of moods;
of angels' moods when they think
they have lost the sight of God.
I think of strength, so strong as
      to withstand the pounding sea.
Of gentle rains upon a mountain
      high, so tall no one can reach it.
Of rage turned loose until it's slowly
      spent.
I think of loneliness so expertly covered
      by smiles.
Of a warm, warm patch of sun amidst
      the cold, cold ice.
Of passions slowly, slowly being
      satisfied.

Outside Your Arms (1973)

I never heard the nightingale
as others hear when they are in love.
For me, time stood still as you held me.
The cricket stopped his violin.
The rain turned to silent snow.
Outside my window, all stood still.
The birds all held their song;
as you made love to me, all else was gone.
Time held its breath; no church bells rang.
I lay locked in your arms.
I never heard the children at play;
never once heard the thunder overhead.
I loved you so that there was never
anything outside your arms.

Endings (1973)

I cannot think of endings.
The end of you and me would be the
end of life.
To face the sun each day would be too much!
And not to ever feel your hands on me—
I'd rather put an end to all!

Those hands of yours give life to me
and I slowly drink from you.
And the days when I can't see you
help only to seep blood slowly back into me,
so as to love you more next time.

I never think of endings;
they will come soon enough.
And when you call the ending,
I will have to call an end to all!

Love Came Late (1974)

When love came, it was too late—
too late to take the pain away.
After a lifetime of waiting, I wasn't his; could never be.

>When love finally came,
>the sun had left my face.
>Love came for me too late
>and he and I shared only pain.

Still, we made day into night
and held each other till we had our fill.
We slept for moments instead of hours
but loved in our hearts on end.

I Light for You (1974)

Sometimes, they seem unending,
the candles that I light.
And they seem to glow forever
and light the endless sky.

Sometimes, I hear the sorrows
of all those lost years past,
and the voices seem unending
and bring the light to end.

I cannot bring an ending
to this life of mine because of you;
without life, I couldn't light
for you the endless skies.

See Me with Your Soul (1974)

Love has only one way of looking:
that's with the soul.
Don't run so fast,
my love,
you might not make it at all.

Stop and see the beauty—
it's there for you to see.
Don't leave out my faults, either;
they might help in the long run.
But please, see me with your soul's eyes.

My Rest (1974)

I want to know, need to feel
that my love to you
is worth a thousand dreams.
       The night, somehow
       just won't let go
       the hectic moments of our love.
I find the wind in pieces
yet, I never loved as I love now.
       Screams rush out of silence
       and in the midst of them,
       I never felt so safe.
To love you is my rest!

I've Come Back to You (1974)

I am back in a world
in which I reluctantly spin;
it is all the sorrows of years past
that so often called to me.

They keep me silent for a while
and that, in turn, keeps me away from you,
and when I find myself serene in silence,
I come back to you.

I've Never Known You (1974)

I need to be alone
with wind and song and you.
To have the time,
time enough to love and talk
and hold you till I'm done.
But time is what we don't have,
and wind never touches us,
and our song is never finished;
of holding you, I'm never done.

My Dreams (1975)

I held the dream just a little bit too long,
until I couldn't tell which were dreams
and which were songs.
      The rivers are all dead,
        yet my dreams keep running, escaping the
        night and mixing with the days.
Sometimes I feel
like the parched earth,
and the leaves of brown,
yet I was never so alive.
And my dreams are never as real
as when I am in your arms.

Love Has Come to Me (1975)

Now at last, I meet the seagull
halfway up in flight—
I love! I love at last!

I now know what the sea,
deep in dark, sings to me—
I never loved as I love now!

I have touched a tear;
I have felt a heart;
at long last, love has touched my heart.

His Eyes (1976)

Oh, eyes that look with tenderness
at him who doesn't love you best!
You look to him with all the love
meant for someone who can see
the gentleness of the heart in you.

Oh, eyes that never cease
to worship him who doesn't love you best.
To look at him like that
can only bring you pain;
oh, heart that loves him who doesn't love
you best!

Let Our Souls Become One (1976)

I run to the top of the hill
because I feel the need to find you.
And I hear only the crying wind;
the mist that hides my very thoughts.

I have no mind to hold onto;
I fall; I become just one more rolling pebble.
The needs become encrusted in the dust;
becoming the very crying wind.

You're not in sun; the mist has taken over,
your needs also screaming, rolling in the dust.
I cannot find you; you need to touch the heart—
two souls now cry, and only you can touch with love.

My mind, now the sighing wind,
I cry now in the shadows of that hill.
Find me; your want is even greater;
let our souls become one in the silence.

Our Destiny (1977)

Travelers, you and I,
in time, although you might not want to be—
but you are locked in time with me.
A destiny that was meant to be.

Please hold me, for I know this much:
I don't know for how long it'll be
until we fulfill our destinies
or death puts an end to one of us.

When in your arms,
I know I love, I live!
Yet, you seem so far away;
the world just stops when I'm out of your arms.

Love (1978)

Oh, no, it wasn't love;
love doesn't hurt at all.
Love gives, it never takes;
it softly holds you in the dark.

It speaks ever so gently.
It never puts you down.
It never has to show off.
It quietly stands aside.

I Loved That (1979)

So full of love for you was I!
Days were pink, nights a cool blue.
My passion grew, and only you could satisfy it.
I who, born between the yellow sun
and the ash of evening when light dies out,
I lived to love you, touch you—
wake to the day with you beside me.

So full of love was I!
That I came to change the darkest of the nights.
I who, born out of the light,
had one way to go—straight into the dark,
changed time around because I loved.

I Am You (1979)

I can no longer breathe on my own,
for my breath comes from yours;
my heart no longer does its vital duty,
for its duty is to you!

My eyes no longer see;
they see only you.
And my body lies waste, useless,
except when it's with you!

We Were (1988)

There was a time when we were stars;
we never cried, we never lied—
we were love, and we were mind;
it gave us all, and we gave all.

We were together with time;
time was us, and we were time—
we were the speed of light,
for light was us.

The music played was us;
for we were music that says all.
We were thunder, we were rain,
and back to it we must find our way.

Lessons in Love (1989)

I came from so far—
traveled eons.
I chose you to come to—
my debts to you pay.

You also had chosen
to come from the past.
The love and the hates
to pay once and for all.

From so far, we traveled
to make right the wrongs.
I chose you, you chose me—
immortal we are.

Don't make the mistakes
that were formed in the long ago.
Change them now, while there's time.
Let's not let each other down.

So far we traveled, so tired we are,
but learn now, the lesson
that love cures it all.
And we'll stop our travels for eons and on.

I Call in Dreams (1990)

I will call upon him who, in dreams,
calls ever so gently to me.
And I will, even in my loneliest hours,
know that he will answer
ever so gently, so kindly, so lovingly
that even angels bow down.

And it is then, that dreams come true—
that humans become gods
and love is now personified,
when he who calls in dreams
is answered by such a lonely one as me.

You Reign Over Me (1991)

We started out a storm!
Raging at each other, yet intrigued,
I wanted you to hurt.
And you, you made me cry.
      And now, oh, how we love!
      The touch of hands on body;
      the gentle voice;
      the knowing you are mine.
And then we try to hurt each other
but immediately forgive.
I know you reign over me,
but I also know you need and
want me still.

Wanderers (1993)

Wanderers, you and I,
in a strange exhausted way.
Because of sentences imposed on us
in the way of love!
> Wanderers, although happy,
> all our duty is to love.
> And yet will never reach the dawn!

For I—the person I have always been—
am hidden somewhere
in the span of time.

And you, not hidden, but always having been,
and out of reach for me,
in a dim-remembered past.

Although with me, a wanderer
> you are!

Of what evil was my sentence given?
What gentle wind did I destroy?
> And so we give love
> and give to each other
> simple pleasures, and try to understand,
> and give without taking, or thought of time or torment.

Forever (1999)

Forever in your arms
is where I want to be.
Forever, with the memories
of a time of you and me.

Until the end of time,
when you and I and stars,
drift away and become one,
and the light we give will be greater than
        the sun.

Loss

No life escapes loss. Loss of loved ones, of livelihood, of faith, of meaning, of things we depend upon…loss comes to all of us.

How we take it in, process it, and live through it is up to us. But trying to sidestep it, to avoid it, or to deny it is not the way to grow through it. We suffer, we weep, we cling…and then eventually, we accept.

Which doesn't mean, at times, we don't still ask why.

Seasons of My Heart (1963)

You were the one who took
my love, my hopes, my dreams.

The seasons came and went
and you were there, I know.
But with each new season,
one last bit of my heart you tore.

How I loved that past that now
haunts me night and day—
a band of gold now holds me to another,
and many miles keep us apart.

The seasons come and go
and you're not here, I know.
But with each new season,
there goes one more bit of my heart.

To a Heart Heavy with Grief (1973)

I had no time to grieve you.
To mourn you was to give myself away.
I loved you so, and you loved me.
But there were others, and they would never see
       our way.
So, slowly, our love became a burden,
and wanting each other so, we had to
       part.
I've never grieved you for anyone to see
my heart heavy with pain.
And longing has never unloaded its burden.
I walk and talk and smile,
and all the time I cry.

Oh, love of mine, I cannot stand this
life of mine; come back!

Eternity (1973)

My love never reached the heights
      that legends talk about;
nor did it ever write a song.
But it was all-consuming,
and it never once asked why.
My love, it never once told my heart
that our love was wrong;
it reached for, it touched, it burned—
it gently loved the night away.
And so, when it was finally all over
and I had lost you, my love,
my grief had never reached the heights.
My grief will never touch the depths.
This pain will never be all over.
It will grow and never reach the heights.
It will yearn and want and love you.
Through eternity there will be no end.

And You (1973)

The sun, the flowers, wind and rain,
all of this and you—
my eyes are full of you
and the wind and stars.
The sky that was so blue
grew dark, and then rains came,
and you, then you were gone.

> All the colors of the rainbow
> surrounded both of us,
> and you, you were the sun.
> But the rains came
> and you, you were gone.

What Was Your Name? (1973)

And the rains came hard,
the lone geranium being beaten
against the window pane.
The blue jay sounds:
is it glad or is it crying?
The rain still falls;
how many have I watched
and cried each time.
I have loved you so long,
have never forgotten your eyes,
but I, in turn, have forgotten.
What name did you go by?

Tomorrow (1973)

Tomorrow, I will say
I did not know that man!
I never once let his embrace
reduce me to shattering glass.

I'll tell the world that he
never meant a thing to me.
That his touch never once
left me begging him for more.

Tomorrow, I will tell the world
I never loved the man.
All those nights of loneliness and want
were only dreams—I never knew the man.

A Life Is Done (1973)

Look up and you will find
our life pictured in the skies,
longing for that feeling that was
for us in the beginning.

      I would follow like a child
and you same as worshipped me.
Just being near each other was enough.

      Time would stand still when we loved.
My heart, strangely standing still now,
looks up at you and our life (pictured in the skies).
My soul feels heavy; my life is done,
for my love for you is gone.

Without Restraint (1973)

(Love will always come)

Without restraint, I came to you.
Without thought, I lay down with you.
I never thought of wrong or right;
I believed love would come later.

But when you love without restraint,
you're bound to lose some in the end.
I always thought there wasn't time;
I didn't give love time to grow.

Life and Me, Together (1973)

I thought of life, and life thought of me.
We came together slowly, each playing our parts.
I lived life to the fullest
and life gave to me itself.

The way I lived it, some never approved,
yet life knew me, and I, life understood.
Fevered by the joys it brought me;
pained by the blows it gave me.

I, exulted by it all,
would laugh with triumph
and cry with frustration,
but I loved it all—lived it all!

Will it Ever End? (1974)

How many years ago
did this night begin?
The nightmares are the ones that laugh;
this night will never end.

      Time was what I never had enough of;
      never enough for you, my friend,
      and I lost you somewhere
      between the evening and the dawn.

I will never sleep again
on this night that has no end.
I shall never see again
those pale blue eyes
that my body fell shy from.
The anger in their blue
cannot be changed to the warmth of those first times.

      The night is now years long—
      will it ever end?
      I face one lover after another,
      yes, for I was never the same again.
      I'm still suspended
      between that evening and the dawn.
      Will this night never end?

Our Love (1974)

I wonder if you ache sometimes
the way I ache tonight.
And if the nights are long for you,
the way mine seems to go on.

I've gone a thousand hours
and gazed at a million stars
and nothing will console me.
The song of love has ended.
See me with your soul.

Love on a Toadstool (1975)

Love was a song
upon a toadstool
and it danced itself around.
Oh! How the sun shone on it,
the love upon a toadstool.

It was sad to watch
when at last the song died down,
the hurt in all our eyes
when love stopped its dance.
And there weren't even memories of a love
that was a song.

The Long Night (1975)

It's now the blackbird's turn
to sing instead of crow.
I don't care to lie—
it's been a long, long night.
And, like the blackbird,
it's now my turn to sing.

While still a baby,
I didn't know where I was;
happy in anyone's arms.
Last night, in a man's arms,
I didn't know where I was.

As a little child, I was never left to stumble.
Now that I'm grown, I fall,
and it's up to me to get around.
I now feel it's blackbird's turn to sing,
but it's been such a long, long night!

Blackbird and I must both find ways
to live, to sing and shout our song.
Blackbird crows;
I don't know where I am.
God, it's such a long, long night.

I Shook with the Force of an Angel (1976)

I shook with the force of an angel taking wing,
and the cry that came from me
was of winds that cried of men's woes.

Tears spilled out in full force to drain the anger
that had risen as I saw them for what they were.

My shame, indignation, the sorrow felt—
their acts, my acts, it all rose,
only to come down on me again.

The wind that at one time died down,
rose in intensity, its shriek the sound of one condemned.
The rain had washed it all away;
the wind, the force, the crying is now spent.

All is gone—we can now read each other's empty eyes.

Across the Miles (1976)

These memories are unending.
Remember me, when you first
set out to fight the day.
Think of me, when you lay down
your head at night.
No matter that there is another at your side;
remember me, and touch with the memories in your mind...
touch *me*, no matter that there is another at your side!

Walk those tree-lined lanes
and know that I am at your side.
Walk in the rain, and you'll feel
I have come to touch you
and you'll lie with me in thought.
Remember me, for I, too, lie in thought.

I walk the lanes and ride the wind.
I lay my body down, to let you touch across the miles.
My heart lies motionless;
the time drags on
But we can touch across the miles.

This Torment (1976)

The night was filled with dreams—
dreams of winds that blew long and hard.
Driven until ageless and limp,
driven of its life gone silent;
driven by the force that was you and me.

Days torment the wind
and the winds torment the nights.
And you and I, driven by a force
strong as stormy nights,
cannot stop the dreams that keep us from our rest.

The Meeting (1979)

Today I stared into the sun
and wished I'd kept my soul
from getting spotted by your song.

Avoid him, they all warned me,
but I saw no wrong, and prayed...
Stay near me, a little longer, stay!

For me, the song is falling.
I have seen and heard enough
to know I've lost my innocence.

I watch you in my memory;
you have no thought of any wrong.
So, in a way, you are God's child.

Where will you be tonight?
What shelter can you take?
I do not fear for you; you are God's child.

While I, my storm is breaking.
Guilt, like ghosts, comes near me.
I fear for me—I know between right and wrong!

Child and Lemon Trees (1979)

You turned and put your hands on me,
and my happiness I could not contain!
I asked you to make love to me;
you said yes, you'd come with me.

Your dear face looked so handsome
I longed to touch it so!
I did, and I caressed it,
and could almost taste your love.

But the lemon trees were in the way,
and I was left to chase a child.
The lemons all had to be picked;
I had to give chase to the child.

My tears started choking me;
I begged the child to stop!
For you were waiting now to love me.
I had to get back; you'd think I'd
         changed my mind.

You waited for me, your longing great;
I wanted to leave the child;
in shocked disbelief, you turned to go—
you thought I didn't care.

I wake to hopeless tears,
to fruitless lemon trees,
your faith and love encased in my mind,
and raindrops being washed away.

My Life (1979)

Of you, I can speak
of your self-assurance, gentleness, and kindness.
Of me, I cannot.
For I search my mind and question my being.
I am one and I am none.
You have found yourself;
I question my very life!

I search for answers heaven-wide.
You're satisfied with every aspect of your life.
I feel when I was giving birth,
the heavens opened wide and cried.
For I cry over something that I lost.

The Angel Made of Stone (1980)

An angel made of stone
now watches in eternal pain.
You, heart, who never had a chance.
       you found your rest, my heart.
       And the angel's sorrow shows
       in its stone-etched face.
Oh, heart, how lonely life was for you!
Love never came to sing its songs.
Yet, you gave when there was nothing left to give.

Oh, God, that took my very soul
and made it sadder than the rest.
God, you took my eyes to see because of how
       they cried for him.
Now under the angel made of stone,
the tired heart lies;
his face shows the pain for all to see.
And he, who never sang with me,
will never come to see
the pain the angel shows
because he knows the soul died for him.

I Cry (1981)

I cry because life took the joy from me.
I tried to laugh and it snarled at me.
When love I tried to have, life
grabbed it and left me pain.
I looked from face to face, and
eyes as blank as death devoured me.
It took half a lifetime to realize
you took all from me!

Your Love Reached (1982)

Your love, it reached the clouds—
and suddenly, it was gone.
>   I stood alone, and listened to the
>   lapping water close to my feet.
I stood there, in my mind, forever,
looked up at the silky night, and saw the
>   stars weeping.

I had lost my heart, now was about to
>   lose my mind,
>   and I saw the stars weeping
>   for all that I had loved and lost.

Dreams that Leave Me Frozen (1982)

I can quit my love
for days while still awake.
For days I can control my mind, my heart.
But nights, my dreams control me,
my mind, my heart.
Dreams hold me spellbound,
praying never to wake up.

They leave me frozen in another time—
a time of you and me.
Of loving arms and lips so warm;
of touching you and you touching me.

I wake because you stopped the love,
the warmth, the dreams I thought would last.

My House (1984)

Without you, I am empty;
there's no one home.
I am memories; an old house
looking out its window pane.

There are hallways leading to nowhere,
and the dust is thick
as the hurt is deep in the empty heart.
And I stand unable to move, like an
old abandoned house.

Futile Dreams (1985)

My dreams of you have become as the spring
     whose flowers refuse to grow.
Oh, dreams! Where do you wish to shed your light?
I am left here all alone and need, oh, need so much to grow!
And you refuse to let me see beyond the dawn.

I know he does not care for me, and I alone
     feel what is known as love.
Give me, oh, dreams, the strength to carry on—
for you, like spring, do not last long;
and I, I must last through winter long.

I'm Sorry (1985)

I'm sorry for the rain
you hated
     and I was never able to stop.

I'm sorry for the things
that made you cry
     and I was never able to stop.

I'm sorry for all those troubles
you had
     and I was never able to stop.

I'm sorry for all those
smiles and laughter I never gave;
because after all of that,
you'd made the happiness all stop.

The Emptiness of My Soul (1988)

It's back with me again,
that feeling in my heart;
the kind the angels get
when they know that God's been wronged.

It's back with me again,
the sadness in my eyes.
The kind only children know
when they know that they're not loved.

It's back, the loneliness
that makes me dream of you,
for it would be the only way
to hold you close to me.

It's back again, the feeling of discontent—
the feeling of knowing there's no one on this earth for me.
Not knowing where to go, what to say—
how to bring you back to me.

It's back again, the sadness and the pain
the knowing nothing matters—
when my heart cannot find rest
and my soul lies waiting in an empty, empty place.

The Mythical Man (2009)

He is like the music I hear inside, and
never put to sound.

He is the sun that comes streaking after a
long, hard rain.

He is all I or you could never put to songs.

He is the light after a long, hard night
and the rest after a very tiring, long,
endless flight.

He is the love lost to all of us
after the daylight comes.

Yet, I reach out and there I touch
him, who escapes us all in daylight.

Anger

How did this terrible thing happen? Why did it happen? How could someone else DO what they did, or FAIL to do what they should have, for and with us?

It is said that all anger stems from fear. The fear? Of loss.

It is a stage in grief, one through which we move as part of healing.

But, oh, the fire of anger can consume all in its path...including us, if we're not careful.

Enduring the heat can make us stronger, if we're wise enough to use it.

You Sinned against My Soul (1969)

I am now far removed from you,
from the soul that is me...
for you lied, and my heart broke.
     And time is not enough
     to bring me back my faith
to bring you back to me who loved!
You sinned against my soul
for your race to love in my life,
     and you will never have the peace
     you had when in my arms.

The World at the End of My Mind (1976)

The world, as I see it spin, at the end of my mind,
its people rolling with the cycles of its sun.
They were too close for comfort
yet so far—at the end of my mind.

I felt their thoughts and turned away;
the world was led by half the strays.
Anger made me cry;
anger took my very eyes.

People in the shadows, aching.
The rain never stopping
to let the stars their light shine.
Leaders stumbled, the frightening never stopped!
The world cries at the end of my mind.

June (1982)

I know what the great minds tell me;
that his soul lives on forever.
But he and his soul are not with me!

His smile that lit up my days,
his eyes that led me on my path.
He and earth and rain
have all become one.
Something I cannot share.

Yes, I know what the great minds tell me,
but I am here,
       and he is where?

Secret November (1996)

Cold and secretive November,
your days are shadows—
how you destroy!
You hold what's left of flowers
in secret places,
in desperate and lonely walls.

Secret November, you have no mercy.
How strange and evil you are.
The jasmine and gardenias,
you take and lock them up—
you laugh at all their cries.

Secret November, I know you have allies,
and when the God of heaven comes, they will be held down.
Secret November, you make innocent hearts cry,
but just remember, I will make you cry!
I will show no mercy to you and your allies.

Alleys of My Mind (1997)

Let me take you to the alleys of my hometown;
They are long, like the alleys of my mind—
long and dusty, save for weeds along the sides.

Come away to the alley of my thoughts,
and, like the alleys of my mind, they are
      long and dark,
save for childhood memories that lie.

Sadness

There is no such thing as a life without sadness, just as there is no such thing as a life without loss.

But how do we deal with the sadness? We can cry. We can withdraw. And we can stop what we're doing in our busy-ness and take the time to look sadness in the face, understand it, and embrace it.

The pause for grief is of different lengths for each person. However long it lasts, if we take it in and don't shrink from it…we will heal.

I Cried (1959)

I cried for the heavens that suddenly went so dark;
also, for the loneliness that lingered so long.
I cried, though your love was still mine,
and prayed to heaven to find out what was wrong.

I cried 'cause no answer was given,
and you could not cease my cries.
I cried for the misery hidden within me.
Never saying, *Excuse me, I'm leaving.*

The Golden Warmth of Sun (1973)

I never asked for the sun itself,
just for a few of its warm rays.
And, in that little patch of warmth,
that you'd be there with me.

The God of love, he never heard my plea,
for neither warmth nor you stood next to me.
The chilling mist, instead, seemed always to be near
and the golden warmth of sun, the winds kept
always from me.

Everyone's Gone (1973)

I want to go home—
to what, to whom?
I have no one; I know no one.

Yet memories haunt me—
they taunt me—
how those dreams laugh!

I want to go home,
but those young, laughing faces
are all gone now, dead.

The Wind's in Pieces (1974)

I felt the wind in pieces,
and your hand you never gave.
It was daisies in the evening,
while robins sang at dusk.

You never saw the wind,
as it streaked while moaning.
Never once returned to silence
or tried to ease the heart.

Somehow the wind is now in silence.
It has stopped its endless call.
Your hand for me seems unreachable,
my heart now wearied by its various songs.

The Crystal Swan (1974)

I had a crystal swan once.
Its beauty was untold.
I never dared to touch it,
but adored it from afar.

The crystal swan stood proudly.
It gleamed in colors bright.
And I only came near it
when the crystal needed a shine.

One day I came to know that the crystal swan could fly;
that another held and loved it,
and the swan was not so strong.
Now the crystal in my heart lay in pieces side by side.

The Frozen Stars (1974)

I called in silent agony,
and no one answered me.
A thousand and one times I called,
and each time, the frozen stars winked from afar.
    The coldness of their icy stare
    I cannot bear another night.

I am no longer free, instead am
    chained to memories.
Your love took all I knew.
I'm left without knowing if
    I had a life before you
    or have one now to live.

I call you now once more.
You do not answer—and I cry.
The frozen stars once more just
    stare.
I am left icy by their chilling
    glare.

Journey (1974)

The journey I must take
is endless, the road a pale blue light.
The rest I need to take, to be prepared,
is undetermined, for I do not know the road's length.

I have memories to take with me
and dreams of heights I did not reach.
I had his love to comfort me,
but time ran always way ahead.

The journey calls to me now—
the clouds come down on earth,
and I alone must start the journey
without his love, without the comfort of time.

Take the Rainbow for a Dime (1974)

Lord, take the rainbow for a dime.
It was never really worth that much.
For a while there, the colors blinded me
to the truth and to thyself.

Lord, take the rainbow for a dime.
The colors are all faded.
It never really had a pot of gold.
It never should have touched your sky.

Heart, Don't Roam in Silence (1974)

Sometimes I hear the sound
of silent storms that roam.
And just outside my window
there's love that wants to call.
      But eyes, misted by tears,
      and a heart that now is cold,
      will not let a hand lift that window
      to let love come to call.
There's a heart that roams in silence,
and it stops for none at all.
It was long ago that it stopped beating,
and it cannot love at all.

My Dreams Are Full of You (1974)

Last night my dreams were full of you
and tender was the touch—
the smiles smiled back at us;
I couldn't leave your side.

Last night you kissed me in my dreams.
It all seemed so real to me;
my hands you held, it all came back,
and you never left my side.

I wake to hopeless tears
and close my eyes to try and see more of you;
to feel the warmth and sweet love of you;
but a nightmare takes its place.

My Tears Become a Raging Storm (1975)

And I spoke to you,
but your mind never reached beyond the silence.
I touched with hands
and their touch spoke for me.

Out in the darkened garden,
the flowers cried out for light
and the dark spoke for me
in the deep that's my very soul;
the tears became a raging storm—
unable to release the words.

That Other Side (1976)

All of them that are dead
were calling me last night;
the hills so green; the past so blue;
their voices gentle; their arms warm.
        I wake to a world of human madness;
        human coldness; lonely, lonely days.
        The days so hot; the sky so cloudless;
        no gentle voices to soothe my hurt.
And those, who for years have been gone,
were warm and kind;
they live in beauty and the hills
are so, so green.

On Crystal Wings (1981)

My heart, it flies
on wings of crystal,
and it hurts when
I try to climb high up in the sky.

My crystal wings, they break
each time I try,
and the pain is more than my
broken heart can take.

The gods keep telling me that
I should try,
but they have not been here
and seen things are like lonely,
lonely stars.

And the crystal wings break
and fall inside my empty heart.

Leaves of Spring (1983)

Come, look at the pond with me.
Its water is green now
from the leaves of spring
that won't let us rest.

Though our hearts are autumn,
let us hold our breaths for now
and gaze at all the new life
that goes on without our care.

Do not think of winter
and what heavy losses we have had.
For our hearts, though heavy with grief,
will, like our souls, go on as if not needing rest.

The new leaves of spring are here.
Winter and all its sorrow is now in the past.
And though we'll never be the same,
there's life in the pond, and a strange new kind of rest.

If I Could Have Loved (1987)

I stood there when things were painful—
stood there and loved them all.
But when things for me were falling apart,
they stood there and felt no love.

I could feel inside my heart—
with my fingers, touch my blood,
and the blood only held
parts of a broken heart.

Oh, if only they had known me
before I became dust, my soul and theirs
would have mixed in colors,
and love would have saved us all!

We Live in Memories (1988)

We live in memories
    both big and small,
like summer leaves remembering
    the ones that fall.

Like winds blowing
    our childish calls.
Memories that creep in dreams
    and we see yellow, white, and gold.

We live in memories
    of little girls
who love the world
    and know not hurt.

Poor little girls, they do not know
    they are just memories to someone old.
Like leaves that fall,
    they, too, are gone!

The Sparrow of My Heart (1989)

The sparrow grows more fragile,
its wings unable to fight the wind;
not able to bear fruit
and too tired to find food.

The sparrow no longer sings
those songs that made us dream,
and it no longer wants to sit on our windowsill
and shiver in the wind.

The little sparrow looks to heaven,
and heaven answers with a thunderstorm,
and sparrow closes its eyes,
a child finds it with a broken heart.

An Angel's Fall (1989)

I'd heard that angels fall,
but I'd never once seen one.
I had heard that they were very beautiful;
what I didn't know is that they were very young.

So very young and beautiful
when those angels fell from grace,
and the thunderstorms that happen
are when all of heaven's sad.

I was told that angels never die,
but I've seen the souls of some,
and I pray that God takes the teenage angels
back into his loving arms.

And Then, I Awaken (1989)

There was a time when leaves were green—
the lakes bluer than the sky.
      There was a child with loving arms—
      somewhere in memory I see this child.

There was a girl whose faith was strong;
she'd sense the good in all that passed.
      This old man talks of a world that's passed—
      he talks of gentleness but his eyes get sad.

This old man tells me of a time
when youth would come and gather 'round.
      When all would visit and laugh with song.
      Where are these young ones he talks about?

Instead, I dream of this little child
as she comes running with open arms.
      She gives me flowers, I give her smiles—
      there, for a while, I know what the old man says.

Only I wake up with sad eyes
and there is never a happy smile.
      And no one's here to gather 'round
      to laugh with song or loving arms.

Despair

The dry points. The desert places in our lives.
These are the stuff of despair.

What saves us ultimately is looking upward from the pit
and realizing there is still light to be seen in the world.
Although the shadows can be deep and sometimes
terrifying, they will not conquer us if we keep moving.

It's just difficult sometimes to take that next step. And then the
next one after that.

Difficult, but not impossible. Deep in our
souls, we resolve to keep believing.

See, Look, Listen (1961)

See, how the wind is aching.
Look, how the clouds are crying.
Listen, the sea is moaning;
hear the pieces of my heart falling.

See the lark, barely flying
Look how the dark creeps in.
Listen, the angels are all crying;
hear the sound of my soul dying.

Love, in Shadows (1970)

Love, it was something in the shadows.
It never touched me, it never gave,
it only took, took from me;
gave to others, never to me.
Let me be lonely, lonelier
than the furthest star.

And because of it, the stars
shine dim, dimmer than
they ever have.

Afraid (1973)

As the morning shadows disappear,
I lie and fear the day breaking.
I begin praying for some dark to stay,
but I never really learned to pray.

I hear rain and am thankful
for a little gloom to stay.
I know there are children in the next room
and they'll soon stir—
and I? I wish my world would die.

I wake to someone else's laugh;
mine is frozen, and I know not
when it happened
that my life became so unimportant.

My Shame (1973)

My arms fell to my sides;
you'd bowed my head in shame.
Defeat was new to me;
I couldn't face the pain.
>The winds had moved the sands,
>the birds were now in flight—
>yet, here I stood, my world had stopped;
>the thread of life had been cut.
The trees turned a soft green;
the flowers showed their blooms—
still, my head bowed down in shame;
I will not face the day.

Search (1973)

My heart is lonely
and it asks a question
to my soul and to my mind.

How long can you go on
with this search for what
you do not find?

My heart is heavy.
It grieves at every turn;
every rock is turned.

Every road is walked;
still, my soul cries.
What do I hope to find?

Pity Me (1973)

Pity me for my hurt.
My grief is heavy;
my wound is deep
and I must bear it!
I have come to nothing.
My joys all scattered,
I am desolate
and inconsolable forever!

I Try to Please Others (1974)

I don't have ways
to say the prayers
that God seems to prefer.

I try my best to do
the things that are right
for me and you.

I go out of my way
to say and do the best
so as not to hurt the rest.

The happier I make others,
the unhappier I become,
and God and others become sad at my distress.

One Heart for Another (1974)

I cried when you left quietly,
but I let my hands hang loose
because what I wanted to touch
was deep in you,
where my hands and tears could not touch.

I cried for you.
The pain and guilt you felt were all because
        of me.
And I cried for me and touched your hair;
my shame could not stop yours.

Memories of Youth (1975)

Youth, like children running past me
  in the park—
it's gone and took the children's laughs,
the very heart to try and catch a bird,
knowing very well wings were not
  for men.

As I grew older, even tears had a different
  taste.
And games were not as innocent as rides
  upon the carousel.
I hid from rain and wind;
only a child would try to play in rain.

I hear a child in play,
because memories never grow old.
And the very heart goes dead in me
to know that's all that I have left.

I Flee (1975)

I flee from you when you are in this mood—
flee back in time, happen upon a place
where I was a child, huddled in fear
of rejection of grown-up moods; of figures
taller than myself.
I do not know where to reach, where to go,
where to hide.
I flee from you, lost because there is no dark to cover me.
Your moods are elusive; I try to understand.
But my fleeing leaves me tired,
my mind blank from all its pain.
The force of your anger leaves me stunned.
I am the child battered in another time,
and I am the woman loving a mixed-up child.
But you are silent, reluctant, too lost in thought
to even want to hear me out.
I flee, happen upon a place...
     where to go...
     what to reach for...
     where to hide!
For I am now a woman, cannot huddle like a child,
the pain somehow a lot more complicated
than when I was a child.

The Door Broke Down (1975)

So, what if I cried again tonight?
I've cried like this a thousand times;
once more won't make that door
break down.

So sad, the cold seems warm tonight.
I turn and find I stand alone;
what if I cried again tonight?

Somewhere in memory, I see a smile
and people gathering all around.
But tears are breaking a home tonight.

So sad, the warm is cold by now.
The tears are gone; the heart is bare.
The home door just broke down.

Leave the Tears Alone (1975)

The tears soon came to a halt,
permanent somewhere behind the eye.
The rose, now crystallized,
        no words need be told—
        they just won't be let out.
        The heart now petrified
        to let love melt its ice.
So leave the tear and grief permanent.
There's just no way to ease the heart;
no way a dead bird's going to come to life,
let alone the rose that's crystallized by pain.

Why? (1975)

Like a person born not belonging to our time
is one who marries not knowing why.

Like a snowbird who ends up south,
you'll wake someday and ask yourself, Why?

The years have passed, there are children now
and, like a small animal, you're trapped.

You run, but run in circles; find there's
not one place to go.

And they all look, think, you've gone mad;
they ask why of you again.

There are countless whys, yet no solutions
to breaking chains that are old and rusty.

Your Heaven (1976)

All of heaven will not sleep again.
Remembering—oh, how they all remember
the beauty of your smile.
I will be in deep rest,
remembering your beautiful love.

I will never be the same again
having heard your love sounds,
remembering your touch.
I and heaven will never sleep again.

Oh, but you will always try to catch the wind
and that makes heaven and I cry.
And I, I try to catch your heart,
but I can't with the wind going by me
with such strength.

Our Prison (1977)

And tears were no longer just tears
but blood rain falling in great sheets.
The safe retreat that was my home,
no longer a retreat but a chamber
with no way out!

And the screech of the owl;
louder than the rain!
My fists pounding the walls
of that airless hall.

And nightmares were no longer nightmares
but plays being played over and over,
keeping the people in their chairs
as they asked, *are they dreams or are
they plays?*

Oh, tears that rose of shame and pain!
And people crying for a retake
of times before the dreams
to keep the dreams from being played;
keeping us from being actors.

The Grave (1978)

Here I lie in frightening darkness
and no one cares.
I, who was always so afraid
to be alone, away from men.

I, in a grave so far
from the laughter and the smiles;
must be here till eternity
and learn to love my grave.

The Brooding Night (1979)

My heart cries out to the brooding night,
but its language I do not understand.
No simpler heart loved him
than this one of mine.
Yet, I'm the one that calls the night.

Whom do I call
when he denies me love?
And night sits brooding and won't answer calls.
Stars? Stars wink back,
but I do not understand at all!

It doesn't matter that I swallow dust,
for what are we but such?
I know he held me once
but it's his spirit that I never touched
and I'm left as barren as the empty night.

I Long for Love (1978)

I whose only ambition is to love—
weary, I trust myself to idle pleasures,
and on my fifth day I fall;
lose hope of ever finding love
and I see the heavens open up and cry.

I am unfinished and unused.
I still have tears to shed.
I am very weary, but I try again,
for all my longings have not come to a rest.

Forever Condemned (1978)

I could wish you songs and music, too,
but dead I lie, and cannot do.
I could give you mine
and give you warmth of love,
>   but I am gone and cold
>   and cannot give you of the song;
>   you here, in the cold rain of the dawn.

Run, run from me.
I am nothing but cold winter rain,
and my wine is chilled to stone.
In the warm love that I promise
is a never-ending trap!
>   And if I promise warm June rain…
…I'll lie, *forever condemned!*

No More (1979)

No more the dew upon my face
or silver stars in my eyes!
No more the sun upon my hair.

No more the young men gather round
to flash their smiles and sing me songs.
No more my heart flies to unknown lands!

The Buried Past (1980)

Bury the past—it can't be done,
for it goes with us wherever we go.
The things done to us, too hard to forgive.
The past comes to us in dreams or other ways.

Leave things behind—easier said than done.
Try to bury them, and it won't get done.
Close the door on them, and the wind will open it,
and leave it all for the world to know.

My Heart Grows Louder (1983)

I wake again in silence;
the birds chirping loudly,
outdoing the screaming in my heart.

I look at the mirror;
I am so small, and feel frightened
to realize I stand on an immense star.

How can I speak to a God who is so big?
In silence, I realize there are suns over my head
and suns beneath my feet.
The screaming in my heart grows louder than
the spinning of the earth.

Rage of an Angel (1990)

She sat there beneath the golden sun.
To take wing at this moment
would have startled even the gods.
She was close to being one of the fallen ones,
for rage was burning in the heart of such a one.

Rage, with all its condemnations
and its alienation from its God,
burned out of control,
feeling anger for those who would not love.

Rage in all its fury, great enough to cause a fall,
fall from grace and fall from heaven,
the soul about to fall apart.
The angel sat in silence, asking help from up above!

For the rage in this one angel
was as black and dark as night,
and since angels do not cry,
all of heaven stood to watch!

The only lonely vigil
was the one the raging angel watched
as it stood and watched them all,
all those who would not love.

(Cont'd next page)

Rage of an Angel, *cont'd*

Those who spoke in fast words,
without thinking of it all.
The angel's fury broke
at their deceit and broken words.

Angels give no warning to the souls on earth
when they are about to strike,
but in that one moment, like a dark, black night,
the angel took away its love and its protection
from all those who would not love.

My Agony (1990)

I have seen stars, and I have lost their sight.
I have run too far, till I lost more than breath.
I have cried too much, my eyes blinded by the tears.
I have died too many times, tired from the strife.

I have been alone too long until I ached too much,
until, at last, my heart has nearly stopped
from the running, the crying, the dying.
And I should sleep tonight, but I wait in darkness; for what?
     For whom?

With my soul left, chilled by its past agony,
my eyes looking back, looking forward,
seeing only empty spaces—empty faces.
My soul goes into dreams, and only then is happy!

To Heal a Wound So Deep (1990)

The bird left memories of songs that
needed rest.
There was no way to revive the bird
that died.
So why even try?

Heart had tears and room
for nothing else.
The strength for words long gone.

Leave alone what time alone can heal.
Nothing's going to heal a wound so deep.

Unable to Give (2010)

My life does not rest in you—
your soul is not my being.
I am no longer significant, even to myself,
and I search endless corridors
looking for my soul.

The only sounds I hear
are the voices of those I've known.
Tortured; looking to possess me once more
but my spirit is running,
unable to give of myself.

Nature

At the end of our frayed ropes of endless motion and strife
— just outside the door — is a miraculous place.

Deep in scented woods…ambling a sandy shoreline…skipping through
fallen leaves…or reveling in swirling snow, we are refreshed on a visceral
level. Stars take our breath away because that's what they're meant to
do: to remind us to breathe in something much bigger than we are.

The world is wide, running on its own internal time clock that
knows not hurry or distress.
In the natural world, what is…is.

As we can simply *be*…and be restored.

Rain (1969)

Love me, the way rain is swallowed up by earth—
tasted, finally drinking all.
Surrounding it with warmth
until again, it asks for rain
the way I begged for you.

Silence, I Need (1972)

I need to stop and watch the butterflies,
but there's confusion all around.

I need to stop and hear the cricket sing,
but there's noise all around.
The need for silence is within me;

I need the gurgling of the brook—
the feel of dark nights to caress me;
to stop and contemplate the cool stare of the stars
and hear the screeching owl.

I need the song of the birds;
to hear the buzzing of insects.

I need the green of grass and trees—
of grass, just under me.
But the bustle of the city
never lets me hear the rain.

Life of the Wind (1973)

The life of the wind is long,
just as my dreams are high.
But my passions are short-lived,
as the different winds pass by me.

The life of the wind is long,
as it tosses back and forth.
It loves to sweep streets clean,
with a strength known only to us.

The life of the wind is long,
and it sees so many dreamers
as it softly blows by us.
Oh, how well it knows us all.

Night Call (1973)

Tonight, I feel like walking in the dark;
touching all my plants in solid dark.
I wish to feel the night engulf me
and all the night sounds talk to me.

Tonight, it seems I hear sad songs;
they sing to me and hope I'll listen.
I want the night to know;
tonight I'll walk and feel its dark.

Seven Winters (1973)

In the dream, I was *so happy*!
and the dream went on and on.
Then I woke and it was winter,
just one of seven winters of my life.

I looked out and it was snowing,
and not a bird I saw in flight.
Instead I felt the cold, cold winter;
just another seven winters of my life.

I thought I heard a child in laughter,
that I felt the warm rains fall.
No, I woke to hear a blizzard
in another seven winters of my life.

I knew spring could be around the corner,
that the warmth of summer comes,
but the stark white of the road ahead
reminds me I have seven winters yet to go.

My Heart Grows (1973)

I see the raindrops on the rosebush leaves—
they're like melted silver drops;
little bubbles dance in the puddles.
Are they infants' tears, or are
they old women's tears?
They're both so frail and real.

The rain falls harder now—
what do we do?
Those who don't know how to cry—
who are too old for tears
and too young to shout out pain—
our hearts grow harder still.

Your Shelter (1974)

I spread my branches wide and low,
stood high above enough to hear the wind.
My leaves shone a bright green;
my roots spread deep and far.
I swayed gently back and forth
to give you rest
       when rest you needed.
My branches draped you
      from the sun,
        to give you cool peace
        when peace you needed.
I moved my branches
        to let you marvel at the stars
        when truth you needed.
I gently hid the light when you preferred
        the quiet of a darkened world.
Birds rested on me, to give you
        song when song you needed.
Come, rest beneath me, and I will
        give you joy.

Too Much (1974)

Today the rain came down—
it shocked me
because the sky looked nice.
>   And now it seems to cry,
>   the day the rain came down.

The geraniums all around my yard—
they seem to think the rain is nice.
Don't they know
>   too much of it
>   will make them rot and die?

Falling of a Heart (1974)

The falling of a heart
in the time of autumn leaves
Left no doubt.
It was meant to be.
       Only one man cried
       for the falling of a heart,
       because he alone knew
       it was more than just a heart.
The leaves fell; died
slowly,
nourishing the earth,
giving life.
       Only one man watched, and cried
       for the falling of a heart
       because it left no doubt
       a man had tried and died.

November (1974)

November is my love,
yet, it makes me cry.
Leaves of green are gone.
In love with November,
still crying in its loss,
I sit and watch the gentle falling of its gold.
November, supreme in its gold and reds,
it leaves me barren of what we had.

Soul Tree (1974)

There was this tree; I loved it so.
It was tall and strong and it seemed it could
stand all the storms!
I loved it and gave my very soul.
I climbed it, and how I loved its song.

     But there were birds and others
     and my arms were not enough.
     And the branches, they leaned—they leaned to
     others with more songs.

I lay, I lay under its shade and its shade
was colder than a winter storm!

     And I knew there was no love that would
warm me or my soul.

Mirrors in the River (1974)

There are mirrors in the river
that go deep and silver shine.
Mirrors of the river;
what you see in them, see in them...
oh, what you see in them.

Look at me—deep I love;
and if you will closely look,
the mirrors in my eyes,
they will, like mirrors in the river,
tell you why; see in them, see in them.

Endless Roads (1975)

My life, it traveled roads
that at times seemed endless
except for a break
down a certain road.

From there it seemed to flow,
ceaseless in its run.
Two different rivers merging
to different restless seas.

The sea was green at times.
Tempestuous and moody was my life,
and always, always running;
flowing out, forever restless.

Your Autumn (1976)

My pain has become second.
It is autumn and the beauty surrounds me.
It is time to put the hurt aside,
fill my being with beauty and strength.
The trees will be bare soon;
the gray will make me sad.
   He will be gone as easily as he came into my life.
And I, through understanding,
will never be the same.
Each and every leaf that falls
must bring beauty and strength.

Dawn (1978)

I woke to find the dawn
silent of birds and silent of songs.
Where was the wind? To what place had it flown?
No use, I would say, once the rain had its start.

I just stared at the mist that gathered so fast.
And the dawn that I'd longed for
was nowhere but in my mind.
For the silence of song was the hush of my heart.

It was silenced for me
in the pitfalls of night.
To again find the dawn,
I must first heal my heart.

Give the Colors to the Rainbow (1978)

How can an emerald seem so beautiful?
Do I have the right to look at it
when there's so much darkness all around us?
So much sorrow, so much sadness.
I find so much in a flower,
in the colors of the rainbow,
but the God I pray to, he seems so
       far at times,
and the help I give to others and to
       nature,
it seems to go undetected.
Give the colors to the rainbow,
to the emerald and nature.
In me there's room for no one—
there's no room left at all.

My Feathered Friend (1979)

Oh, feathered friend of mine,
don't sing in the rain too long.
You might find in the spring
you will be unable to take a drink!

I see how you can love those musical silver drops
and what utopia you feel
flying in beautiful fine mist.
But in the spring, you'll
be unable to take a drink!

One Day I Will Fly (1982)

Birds flying in the distance
break my heart in two,
for they fly to far off places
where I know I'll never be.

Birds fly with no permission
to places that I'll never see,
and they talk to one another
of places yet to be.

I sit here in lonely shadows
with no one to talk to me,
but someday my soul will travel
faster than those birds will ever do.

Emptiness of the Dawn (1982)

No one to feel the emptiness,
no one to ease the soul.
Like the night owl
forgetting the dawn,
he flies over dreams known.

Daylight burns on one's face,
and faces are barely visible
in the brightness of the day;
days we run away from like the owl
runs from dawn.

Autumn's Victory (1985)

The leaves of green
        I could not hold or stop;
they turned to autumn colors,
        and now they're gone.

I look up at the tree and wonder
        how it, being so tall and strong, could
lose its small green leaves
        and not find a way to hold them.

So sad, the tree that stands there—
        so sad, the leaves are now gone.
Together they could have made it,
        and their song they could have shared.

First Leaves of Fall (1983)

Come, look at the leaves of fall;
they tremble now, thinking of how soon they'll die.
They hang on desperately,
watching the first ones fall.

They think of the wonderful summer,
yet tremble to think of the snows ahead.
They look down, seeing the first ones on the ground,
their gold and yellow now a faded brown.

Happy are the first leaves that fall;
they do not have to stay and watch
and remember soft breezes and coats of green;
they do not agonize with the last of the leaves of fall.

Come, gaze at the leaves of fall with me.
They are more beautiful in death
than when they were first born
to the trees of spring.

Leaves of Summer (1984)

Come, walk in the woods with me.
All the animals will stir
the way my heart stirs with strange feelings
when I'm with you.

Come, the trees are so green
from the rains that fell,
the way my heart is full
from having met you.

Come, listen to the music of the wind
as it softly touches the leaves,
the way my soul sings
when you gently touch me.

I Know the Wind So Well (1985)

How does the wind feel
when it rustles through the trees?
And what does it think of you and me?

I know the wind, and I know just how it feels;
and I know that when it wails,
      it just tries to hide its pain.

I know the wind when it is playful
and I know that when it wails,
      it just tries to hide its pain.

I know the wind when it is playful
      as it plays with your hair.
I know how much it wants to be held down
      in someone's arms.

Oh, I know the wind so well
for it is a reflection of myself.
Oh, when will the wind and I
find the one to hold us down?

Alone in the Dark (1985)

I once wrote about a garden,
a garden that rose out of the dark.
And in that garden I made flowers grow;
I gave them life and colored them with song.
Now I look around for my garden;
I guess it's autumn and I don't know—
for there's nothing there; the color is gone!
It's me alone, standing in the dark!

My Winter Rain (1985)

The sound of winter rain:
its subtle sounds speak of pain.
Out of my window, I see soft drops dance,
and I know for too long,
I joined in its painful dance.

I must stop the winter rain—
it doesn't help to brighten our day.
But how can I catch and change its way
when I sometimes think of myself
as the saddest of all cold winter rains?

Echoes of Children (1987)

There were flowers in a garden
that would grow as tall as trees,
and the birds would dance there in the morning
and then again at dusk.

They would drink of the fountain
that stood there just for birds,
and the trees would sway and whisper
how much they loved it all!

There were children, and their laughter
would ring out twice as strong
as the wind among the pine trees
that stood so very tall.

There were friendly insects
like the tiny ladybug.
And it was a sad, sad morning
when the garden grew no more.

The Tears in Your Eyes (1987)

What can we do when the sky
chokes up in pain
and won't let its tears—the rain—come down?

It wasn't right, my friend,
to let the star there lose its light,
and now a permanent tear lies
there somewhere in the cold of my eyes.

The sky chokes up in pain
and there's nothing we can do.
The tears have turned to glass
and I can no longer see your side.

Soul Travel (1988)

There was a time when swans were golden
and birds a silver white,
and we would streak across the skies
in shimmering golden lights.

When we stopped and talked to stars
and raced with comets for their light,
and trees would give off colors
like rainbows give to us.

We loved to show our love
and come to earth to see
the creatures God had blessed
and given them to you and me.

The Rose (1988)

The rose today spoke to the oak tree;
it asked the tree where it got its strength.
The oak did not answer; the rose was so small.

The rose trembled, the thunder was so loud,
and the thunder laughed and grumbled
to see the rose turn white.

Inside the rose, a small pink started;
it gathered strength somehow,
but it was gone when dark clouds rumbled.

And the angry rain came down—
poor little rose was battered;
its petals all fell off.

Too late, the rose is gone.
Not one of them cared enough;
still, stems and roots are there; maybe someone
        will care enough to carry on.

Winds of the Past (1994)

The sadness of certain hours
has determined my hours—
bringing with it cold beginnings
to those times I could have loved.

I know the way the wind blows,
and why it cries a mournful song,
and when I see the bird fly,
I know which way it wants to go.

I know the wind now has a different sound
than days ago, when I was just a child.
It appears it now blows more angrily
than the melody from when I was young.

To Capture a Star (1994)

She wanted to capture a star,
a star that would fill her with light
that would take her to places she knew she could find;
a star that would help her to soar
to places filled with love and light.
But the stars kept their distance,
too far for her eyes to find.
She knew she never could fly
to those mystical places afar.

The Sound of Rain (1995)

How sad the sound of the rain.
So very sad, that we retreat behind closed doors,
afraid, afraid to hear the sounds within
       our own hearts.

The rain pounding at our window-panes
makes us wonder if God is calling our names
as we wrap our arms around ourselves, afraid.

Come, Let Me Show You (1996)

Come, give me your sadness,
for I know just how you feel.
Put your sadness in my hands,
for I am stronger than you think.

Don't let your dreams torment you;
give them to me, for I know
I can hold them and erase them
and make the storms of darkness pass.

Come, let me show you
how worlds are made and worlds are lost,
and how stars that seemed to have died
are stars that have just been born.

Desert of My Soul (1998)

I, the dry, empty desert,
blow and howl in the wind.
Rains do not come to me.
The way to win strips me bare.
      I call out to the sky
      and it hears not what my heart wants.
The suns burn me—
and they blame me for the dry sands—
and nights I am cold, so cold;
they say some die in my coldness.

I'm dry, but in emptiness.
And the wind howls my loneliness,
and though they have died in me,
there is life for many in my sands.

Dreams of Greed (1999)

There were flowers in my dream—
they were red, how they shone.
They would rise as high as oaks,
and they rose out of the ocean.

Then I reached out to embrace them;
lost to everything but the brilliance of their glow.
I found my dream became a haze;
the flowers were not there.

What was it they tried to tell
when they glowed their brilliant light?
Why can't I live my life without
the glow, the light, the heights?

Soul Owl (2007)

I, and that soul I never met,
like two young owls hidden in the dark,
our haunted voices hidden in the moon.

If I could tell that other soul
how much I've needed the closeness of its light;
the light to shine my aching, lonely nights.

I, who never met that soul so like mine,
would hold my hand and I, his heart,
but two owls remain hidden in the dark.

The Cat Who Wanted Wings (2012)

He was a merry thing;
he was too fat for such a cat—
he was the cat who wanted wings.

Wings are not given to foolish cats;
they might just fly away, and
who will catch the rats?

Oh, the cat who wanted wings
hoped he'd sprout wings
and that it would soon be spring,
because that is the season
for little birds to try their wings!

But, like I said,
he was too fat,
and if he doesn't chase rats,
the rats will be the ones
who will get fat.

He sat on a branch
in a backyard tree
and tried to tweet…
but only a meow would come.

Bitterness

When someone wrongs us, it leaves a dank residue on our hearts and spirits. When a guilty party seems to continue through life unscathed by their own wrongs, even while we are scarred, we cry out that it's "not fair."

It's not. But, then, we already know life isn't "fair."

Glorious, tragic, mundane, ecstatic, soothing or jangling — life can be myriad. "Fair" is a different construct entirely, narrow and binding, a stealthy poison to which we cling at our own peril.

When the scales do balance, we are in rare air. When they don't, we need to step back, recollect, and draw our feet back from the darkened ledge.

Weep (1964)

Weep till your heart has no tears left.
Weep till all your sorrow's gone.
Weep till you're sure you won't cry anymore.
Weep till your heart won't love anymore.
Weep till you won't feel anymore.
Weep, heart, weep, but make sure no one
    sees you cry.
For no one's worth your tears; no one's
    worth your cries.

Affairs (1973)

I've met men and been in love
with each and every one.
And, at the end of each affair,
been through the hell, the tears and pain.

I have told myself before each one
that I've never been in love
and have told each man in turn
how he, to me, was number one.

I have laughed each time I see
how each thought himself so manly,
thinking how he, at last, had made me
fall in love for the first time.

You're Laughing at Me, God (1973)

Now you're laughing again, God,
at my weakness and my pain.
You seem to laugh the hardest
at my trust of you and man.

You seem to love the way
my dreams all fall apart.
You're laughing again, God;
I have fallen for his lies.

His Shame (1977)

I see the prisoner
handcuffed, in silence,
head bowed, eyes down,
as they take him down the hall.
What are you thinking,
you, who know what he has done?
That he is evil?
Or is he evil because
he was too gentle?
You, who walk him down the hall—
are you the one that's free
because your heart was not as gentle,
and life and others never pushed you
till you ended up like him—
eyes looking down, head lowered in shame?

The Pain of Light (1978)

I took one step toward the sun and
backed away from the light
because I found sun and light
were not the same.

I walked away from the darkness of my room,
out to the darkness of the night;
the night I found overwhelming,
my room a burned-out star.

And I knew life to be one big game,
the only difference were the players.
and the jokes they liked to play
but the games were all the same.

Our Dreams Died (1982)

We have spent ourselves dry—
thinking of what we should have said or done,
not really caring if we did or not.
Leaving our homes to rot, our trees to die,
our children no longer seeing us as once
        they had,
but as people they would rather not
        know at all.

Yes, we had dreams; they lie in graves now.
Our hearts no longer young, only bitter, laughing
        at love, or those who love.
We stare empty-eyed, and care not to sleep
        at night.

Days are spent thinking of ways to run
while flowers in that once precious garden die,
and June becomes the coldest month of all.

They Never Let Me Know (2003)

If anyone heard the songs I sang,
no one ever said they did.
If anyone listened to the dreams I had,
they never once let me know.
Yet, I knew their songs
and heard them talking in their sleep at night.

So why is it that no one heard my cries?
And I had to look for a stranger to ease
the wanting left inside?

Reflection

Sages tell us a life without reflection isn't worth living.

Moment by moment, whether we are aware of it or not, we reflect.
We make decisions, determinations, destinations.
We discern the difference
between fear and prudent caution, between
temporary impulse and true instinct.

We refine even ourselves in a crucible, seeking the essence that
makes us who we are.

Put it Away (1959)

Put it away,
they say about love
that has not worn well
or lasted long.
Put it away,
like yesterday's glove,
or a tune that was never played.
And so I have;
I've put it away.
Its ghost just rises
now and then,
when no one hears
and no one speaks,
like a wounded child.

I'll Climb That Mountain (1960)

I'll climb that mountain, no matter how high.
With my love I'll melt its size.
No matter how majestic, it will bow down.
And with my love, it will not die.

I'll climb that mountain, or else I'll die.
With my love it will come alive,
and ice will melt dry,
to love me forever or else both of us will die.

Will I Be Okay? (1970)

Where am I going
when I don't even know where I've been?
How do I introduce myself
when I don't know who I am?

How do I tell myself
everything is all right
when I don't know if all right
comes my way?

I Had a Feeling (1972)

I have a feeling you will be
one of my very best memories.
Not one of hurt or looking back,
reflecting utter feelings of loneliness.
Although you must be gone from me,
I must let you go.
You will, with me, leave memories.
And looking back, will I just smile.
I'll think and say, I had a feeling
that he would leave me my very
best warm memories.

Dark Moods (1973)

Life itself seems to be brooding.
Dark moods that set us all apart.
I try to set my roots down somewhere,
but rains have washed them out again.

Growing passions brought by pain
have placed me elsewhere again.
Guilt to darken more my moods.
Restless search for wants unknown.

The heavens brood—
I feel their disapproval,
and still my passions rise—
my restlessness is wide.

My Ghosts (1973)

I hear ghosts rustling about;
I almost hear their pleas,
the pleas that go unheard,
the tears that go unseen.

Could I but just reach out
and comfort an unheard sob?
Reach out and wipe one tear
that an eternity can't dry.

The ghosts just pass me by.
I'm just as guilty of
not hearing sobs or cries,
and so, they pass me by.

My Loneliness Grew (1973)

And the rains came, they caressed me;
my loneliness just grew
—I grew and grew, tall, tall, so high
I reached the sun!
       It, too, caressed me.
       My loneliness just grew.

Shadows, so many shadows!
Elusive, they dart and hide;
I hear a song, it reaches for me:
I can't touch you yet—oh, the loneliness!
Wait! There's movement; it, too, is swift.

And I see you in the distance
reaching out—extending—growing, tall-tall-tall!
You're reaching to the sun;
it is devouring you.
My loneliness is *wide*.

My Great Hate (1973)

My great hate would not let me
lift to anyone a helping hand.

My hate, it made me be
something I never wanted to be.

My hate, it lifted me, it carried me
to what? I couldn't tell!
It taught me what to say and see;
it taught me how to hurt and be.
Love anyone? My hate would not let me.

My hate kept anyone from loving me.
Strength, my hate did teach—
or so I thought, when I never fell apart.

My hate for sure taught me to walk
because alone is how I've always walked.

My hate was everything to me;
it taught me how to feel.
How could it be the things I did
that I never wanted to do?
I never smiled.

My Great Hate, *cont'd. next page*

My Great Hate, *cont'd.*

My hate, it never let me be.
My hate, it made me stand apart
from those with whom otherwise I could be close.

My hate, it seemed to grow,
and very much alive I knew it was.

My hate and I were very close;
we never needed anyone.
And now that I am all alone,
my hate just rises now and then.

Other Ways of Love (1973)

You're teaching me new ways to love—
new ways to sort my mind.
The things you say to me
I know are to arouse the sleeping me.

Some of the ways you love me
I know are fine and good.
How could it not be right
to love the way you love?

But other things you say—
other things you do—
are meant to shock and disillusion
the freshly awakened me.

Why would you love me so,
then do the things you do?
Could it be you know just how I feel
and want me to run from you?

Mind's Passages (1973)

In my mind, there are passages,
and the whisperings I hear
are quite unbearable as a threatening sphere.

In my mind's passages,
hopelessly bound are secrets and guilt
that time has not healed.

I destroyed all his wanting and need
and he no longer smiled when near me he came.
How strange that my mind should think of him at all!

Time Is Drifting (1973)

I seek the sun
and wish to find some warmth.
I become sad; there is none.
        I seek out trees
        with green extending
        the comfort lost in their dead branches—
with words and actions
I wish to tell you
that time is leaving; dusk drifting in.
        But, like the tree that stands so tall,
        some love its green, some seek its shade.
        Still others find and hear the message.

Back in Time (1973)

Last night I went back
to the time of shaded trees,
of quiet farms and life so sweet.
      And in my waking days I left all this
      for steel and concrete;
      empty faces and faceless streets.
The senseless worlds these people live in;
the loveless words they use
and so they artificially get high.
      I, at least, will save myself.
      Go back to the time of shaded trees,
      of quiet farms and life so sweet.

My Restlessness (1974)

Oh, mind, what do you want from me?
I have no thoughts on it all!
I do not wish to think at all.

Soul, why do you roam?
You seem to find no peace at all.
Don't look so sad; you let yourself find rest.

Spirit, why can't you pull yourself together?
Why let the wind toss you around?
I'll never be back at your side!

What Became of Him (1974)

What became of him after he died?
Did the ocean take him in?
Or does he in the eagle fly?

What became of him? I'd like to know.
Does he ride the night wind?
Or walk the endless roads?

Does he next to God abide?
Or here on earth his spirit stride
to watch what's left of him behind?

My Song (1974)

I am rising slowly
up in a cloud of yellow smoke.
All around me I see faces
and voices calling—whispering.
Some extend their hands, but
I only see the ones that stay back.
I am drifting, and the calls,
they grow dim now.
I see many places
I've never seen before,
hear many songs I never
heard or ever sang.
I can now touch all their minds.
      I know all their questions, too.
Still, I am so far, too far for
      anyone to hear my song!

Midnight Ann (1974)

Midnight Ann, they called her;
she'd light her candles in the night.
Out in Detroit; up in New York, and back down south,
their glow you'd see.

Midnight Ann—she's gone now,
but the candles still remain.
You can see their glow in the forest
and in the darkened skies;
you can also see the candles down some lonely city street.

Yes, Midnight Ann remains.
We all see her glow there still,
because Midnight Ann has lighted
many, many a stormy night.

What Will I Do (1974)

What will I do after you are gone?
After our pitiful few moments
are no longer there?
Funny how thoughts like these
can break a spell
and, for a moment, take the joy.

I know now the difference between feeling and touch;
between loving and caring;
between passion and simply wanting.

What will I do after you are gone?
Now that I can give without having to take
and love without question of why or when.
Let me now give all the love I can
and make you feel our moments
are worth a lifetime of pain.

I know so well we'll have to give each other up,
and that the day grows closer each new dawn.
But let me love, talk, sleep, touch, feel—
all in the falling of a leaf's time.

To Feel (1974)

When was it I woke up
to find that I was changed?
That I was not content
merely to see,
but wanted to be able to touch—
to feel—
to feel!

Not wanting to wake up
and stand in second place,
I lay a moment longer
and thought of ways to change.
And, most important,
to be able to listen
when all of us were talking.

Don't Question Me (1974)

Don't ask me any questions;
I do not have the answers.

I see the earth shaking,
and it cries for something lost.

But it has friends somewhere
and it's up to us to let them help.

Don't question me on my answers;
just read the signs. They're there—
look with your heart.

Change (1974)

Time itself laughed as the daffodils danced.
The change that took place
took my very breath away.
My heart, strangely still.
I, standing in change;
the soul remaining the same.

Yet, change taking place
without pause or shame.
And we, all standing still
and very well knowing
we would never be the same.

I Do Not Want to Hear (1974)

As I enter silence
with the past still talking to me,
I will not let its voices taunt me
as do nights when rest can't come.

I am now deep in solitude;
love dares not touch at all.
I will not let your voice reach me.
It would only wake up sounds I do not want to hear.

The Talking Tree (1975)

They thought to stop the child within me.
They all came to the hanging of my soul,
and I could hear their swearing.
It seemed to fulfill what they
were searching for,
at the hanging of my soul.
No sooner had they attempted to rid
       the soul of child,
that a voice was heard from the tree I was under:
the child will always take another form,
and it will always be, until in it,
all of you delight.

My Youth Is Gone (1975)

Because time always ran ahead
too fast, I never saw the sunset.
And the earth, spinning endlessly,
never let me hear its songs.

Youth to me was a crown.
Just another of life's gifts to me.
I took it lightly, thinking it would always be—
but there was time, running, always running.

Came to find my youth was gone one day;
that I was left further back
than a spinning world could find.
Funny how all my dreams were still the same.

I, the Silence (1976)

Again, I become the silence
and the silence becomes deafening,
shocking everyone to screams.
I was laughter at one time;
I could ring out with delight.
And the sun behind the smiles
is now dark silence all the time.

Leave me one noisemaker—
the one the child is holding now.
Let me try, help me to break the silence;
for my heart has no more songs—
not one song to play at night.

Strange Memories (1976)

All those strange hours that you and I spent,
a puzzle because we never spoke of the heart.
Now, those hours lie in suspended time.
But where do we lie? We won't see each other
between screaming odd sounds,
or needs without sounds.

Where was the start and where was the end?
Where are all those strange hours—
they don't die, the need and the want;
the memories are carried, never once dropped.
Even in sleep, the memories are never lost.
You will cry, because they are your strange memories.

Silent with Thoughts (1976)

I feel the silence
as my bare feet lead me
to one thing after another.
My thoughts on you,
my being full of hurt,
wondering how one can be
so unaware of another's pain.
Sounds, they all become one.
And I find myself one
with the silence.
Silent with the thoughts
that have no answers
and the need that has no escape.
I plead, but to the silence,
and I get no answer.
Why should silence answer silence?

What Is Life? (1977)

What is this thing called life
that ties me, that takes my sleep?
It makes me run, it makes me shout.
It makes me happy, it makes me cry!

What is this thing called life
that makes me angry, that makes me love?
It takes my breath away: it leaves me stunned!
This thing called life.

What is this thing called life
that makes me wonder?
It makes me turn around.
It makes me curse, it makes me pray—
too much, too little, this thing called life!

I Need (1977)

I need the mist of heaven
to touch my body gently.

To have God's eyes
look down on me; I need compassion.

I need to hold a bird,
one that understands my flight.

I need the warmth of lips and arms
that know how rare it is to love.

I need a heart that cries for me
because it knows how I, too, cry.

I need to know you look and love
with your soul's eyes.

Tonight (1977)

Tonight, I feel so tired,
like ground-drenched days
by endless mist.
        The comfort of the fireplace
        is lost; I need rest,
        and talk must wait.
Memories of home crowd in.
Thoughts of when I was a child,
being able to talk the day into night.
Tonight I feel so lost,
like God must feel
when he loses one of us.
Still, rest evades me, and weary, weary
is the child in me.

Where Is This Child? (1977)

Somewhere, I see an upstairs windowpane,
pelted by raindrops in the evening haze.
And looking out, with long blonde hair,
a girl of six or eight!
> I hear her sobs and feel her pain;
> in loneliness she looks at rain.
> The trees groan with the heaviness of rain
> as her memories are heavy in her heart.
Somewhere, somewhere, I see this child.
I need only to reach out!
But if I should reach,
would that child be me?
And the ghost of her would tear my heart apart!

Those Sounds (1977)

I don't look at shadows
lying there alone;
the shadows look at me!
And, outside my window,
the crickets sing to me.
Sad, sad silence
holds every corner of my room
and I feel the odd sensation
of life standing still in me.

Should I be out in crowds?
But how does one empty out sounds?
Sounds that only happiness can bring.
The dawn shows itself near
the shadows, looking more
like ghosts now.

The Woods I Call My Self (1978)

The haunting, sad melody of a piano.
A piano I never played.
The songs I never sang for anyone to hear.
Why, then, the yearning, the feeling I've played
and sung somewhere before?
      And he and I love in dreams
      as if I've lived through him somewhere.
      Yet, he evades me in the waking dawn
      and it all empties up my soul.
      If life is not a part of me,
      why, then, am I a part of life?
Why do I run so fast and yet—
stand in the same dark place?
What is it I give to others
that I never give myself?
I remain empty, lost in the woods
I call my self.

Revelation (1978)

I thought I knew you
and, sad, I thought I knew myself—
and the world I thought I knew so well!

But you and they, you didn't give me time.
I spoke in hushed tones
and I walked alone.

And in my dreams I, I lost myself.
The world and you had lost me long before
I started to care—care about myself!

Oh, Life! (1979)

Oh, life, what do you want from me?
You offer love and shelter,
but only for a time.

The green of trees you give to me
are only for the summer.

Oh, life! Why do you give me love,
then take it the next moment?

And why the sullen moments
when I'm not sure you're here at all?

Made of Glass (1981)

I tried to tell you, make you see
how some of us are made of glass.
Some flowers feel the biting wind
while others dance with it.

I've often wandered into valleys
with only silence by my side,
and the songs I sang were never heard.
You came to find that glass is what we're made of.

Yes, us, we who kissed in the dark—
who walked at night and only heard
the cricket, the bullfrog, all the night sounds—
we found that we were made of glass.

We found that in the dark,
we can so easily slip and fall.
And, knowing we are made of glass,
can break so easily in the dark.

The Truth within Me (1981)

I searched for truth outside myself
but never found one hint
of what my heart desired.

So I let go of truth
and things that stand outside of love
became, to me, my great escape.

I lost my soul, my very being,
and truth no longer mattered;
I went outside myself.

I did not travel far enough,
or so I thought I had to—
when truth was all the while inside myself.

I Need to Fly (1982)

I want to fly, and be in arms that never lie;
to be with someone who tells me there
is no such thing as pain.

I need to see him who died on me
and ask him why?
That I did love, and yet love was never
quite enough.

I need to let the world see
they are not, not one of them, like me!

You Loved (1988)

It isn't you that love has left—
it is love that has lost itself.
Like snow that gives so much joy
must melt when the warmth comes.

You, you know how much you have loved,
and they did not know,
how much of you the world knows—
how much of love you know and the world did not know.

The Soul (1988)

Does the soul age?
      I don't think so.
Because the soul cries like a child,
      no matter what your age.
It feels a loneliness
      like a child who's lost.
And it feels as strongly
      as a youth without a home.
I know, because the dreams
      are still the same
as when I was a child;
      the soul just wearies; it never ages.

My War (1989)

Tonight, I think of them again;
my war is over,
and I find no peace.

I fly to heights they'll never know
yet, know I never rose above the ground.
How could I? When love was to be the fuel to take me off.

The war has ended, I fear and hope;
disappointed, I trust no one,
and match the wind in its loud cry.

The burning in me is now out;
I am now frozen like the ice.
I know of war but not of peace.

I think of them again tonight
and know they do not think of me.
Dear God, *their* war has *just begun*!

When No One Claims Your Heart (1989)

She didn't die when the thorns pricked
      her finger;
she died from a lack of roses in her arms.
      She didn't die because angels came for her
but, rather, because angels didn't
      come to call.
She reached out so many times
      and love stepped back
so as not to want to love.
      She died because she had
      seen someplace, somehow.
She didn't die because her heart was
      broken
but, rather, because no one ever claimed her
      heart.
She didn't die from lack of love
but, rather, love betrayed.
Today, she tried again to reach out;
they didn't see or hear her,
so she died.

A Thought (1990)

How many stars did I try to reach?
To hold one in hand and ask of it
the same questions
that I ask of men!

The need to share a human mind—
make it receptive to the needs
of indiscriminate thought
and love only freedom that he can share with others.

The Hours (1993)

The hours, weary of the day,
drift gently into the lonely night.
The endless bitterness of day
can be absorbed in dreams.
Until it's time once again
to begin the battles of another day.

The night hours sleep in endless waves
of simpler times, of childhood plays.
Of tender parent who cradles hurt away,
of warm fire and warm beds.
The hours, weary of the day,
drift into darkness, so aware
of tender moments spent in childhood prayer.

My Fear (1999)

I saw the hills;
>> I did not understand them.
And the forest, it was dark;
>> and I was frightened!

I tried to speak;
>> they did not listen.
And the moon, it dimmed its light—
>> it made me stumble.

I walked, so far
>> I lost my way
and could not get back in my heart;
>> and once again, they did not listen.

Where is my soul?
>> My pain has driven it away.
I turn and they are
>> in that dark forest I fear so much.

Leave, the hills tell me.
>> They do not love you.
Do not speak, they will not listen.
>> Just go, your heart and soul will find you here.

Run (2011)

The moon is so erratic
it has lost its quiet watch.
We have lost the ability to care
and don't even remember its light.

The owls seem so scared;
they tremble in their nest.
The animals all hide
and cover their little ones.

The woods grow darker
and I seem to lose my way,
but I can't stop, I must go on;
I can't let the ones around me stop my run.

Warmth

As babies, we are swaddled in warmth.

As children, we crave sunshine and hot chocolate.

As adults, our warm serenity comes from opportunities
around us — in giving of ourselves, in basking in the
glow of true friendship and the ardor of love, and in those
serendipitous miracles that surprise even the child in us.

Warm moments are worth their weight in gold; we tuck them around
us when chill winds of hard times or difficult situations threaten
to abrade our bones.

And we smile, taking a deep draught of a serenity that only
grows sweeter with time.

Secrets of the Wind (1960)

How silent and majestic the trees are.
How beautiful their song can be.
How many secrets each tree holds
and whispers it as the wind blows.

Search Ended (1961)

I walked the river road in search of God.
I looked across the river and up above the clouds.
Everything was quiet; not a sound I heard,
as if God resented my questioning him.
But I had to find out why, if there was a God, I felt so lost.
I looked all around me; I saw only river,
road, trees, and sky;
still not a sound I heard.
Then a bird above me flew, a fish in the river jumped, and
a breeze made the heat go.
I lifted my eyes to the heavens and saw the rays of the sun.
I whispered a prayer of thanks; knew that now at last,
my search had ended.

The Cricket Sings My Song (1973)

Last night, the cricket sang my song.
He knew exactly how to sing my love.
He said the night was long,
and how the day glares on and on.

Last night, the cricket sang my song.
It told how much of life he'd seen,
and how much a part of it I'd been.
It sang of sorrow and how often we all stand alone.

The cricket knows my song.
He sings it evenings, now that I am gone.
The cricket searches for what I left behind—
I live in him; he sings my song!

Ahead of Life (1974)

Don't walk so fast, my friend;
I seem to lag, always, two steps behind.
You and life seem to stroll and then run, my friend.
And I stay back, unable to catch up.
Walk, my friend, beside life;
let it show you its joys, its trials,
but wait for me; I'll soon catch up—
in good time, all in good time.

Today, I said so much I never said before,
and deep in me, I knew I'd taken
one more step.
I did, for you, what I never dared before.
Reach out your hand, my friend.
Life's waiting for us both
and we can run together—
ahead of life!

Faces of the Past (1974)

They're calling me tonight—
my childhood friends,
their voices young.
They're all now scattered
far and wide.
Yet, their shouts of joy
ring loud and clear!
       Norma, with her golden hair;
       Anna, with her soft brown curls;
       Antoinette, who vowed she'd be a nun,
       and Velma, with her dark, mysterious eyes.
Minerva, with her green, clear eyes.
Dolores, with her dreams so high.
       Their faces all come back to me
       and I wonder how they think of me.
       Do they see me shy or wild,
       or that I could dream as high?
Do they think that I could smile,
and had a dream or two within sight?
Do they see my face and hear my voice?
I wonder if, to them, I was ever a child.

Patience, My Heart (1974)

Sit alone and keep silent, my heart;
the hurt will not last long.
I know you feel grief now,
but you will not lie in the dust for long.

Sit alone and remember none of it, my heart;
the time for smiles will come.
I know how very lost you are,
but you will come out shining—believe me, heart!

Moody Rain (1975)

I almost hug sounds to me;
the sound of rain,
soft or angry, but sad,
always sad.
I hug the sound of insects, insistent, lazy,
going on with their own lives.
The happy sound of birds
scolding, wondering about me.
And the sound of the wind,
with its soft cry or its shrieking wails.

Moody rain, whispering to me,
speaking of darkened skies from
where it comes.
Birds now silent in their shelters.
I hug the sound of faraway thunder
like hugging the past strongly.
And the moody sounds renew my soul.

The Sea (1976)

I never saw the sea
as I did this last summer,
wearing beautiful greens and blues,
and its waves, gently rocking back and forth.

The sand was never clearer,
the water never warmer;
The sea was never more beautiful—
the summer I turned ten.

Thoughts (1976)

The thoughts come on restless nights.
And when days lie still,
no storm can touch me
when thoughts reach out to me.

They can become words that ring
out from voices long gone.
They can touch and sing
and give you hope when you are down.

My Heart Sings (1979)

I think the birds have
all gone mad,
the way they sing
on this spring day.

It seems that all their friends
received a special call
to come and sing
in my backyard.

They know my lover's golden hair
is mine to touch now every day.
That his blue eyes now light my path,
and his strong arms keep me from shame.

My heart now sings as much as theirs.
My heart now flies on wings as they.
My lover now gives me the rest
my soul had lost when once astray!

I Was (2003)

It was the leaves of spring that made me laugh
and toys and flowers were all around me.
The leaves that were bright green, were for me—
all of them, just for me!

It was in summer when things were great;
when everything that was, was in my lap;
when the brightest of the stars would actually
come down
for me to just reach out and touch!

It was in fall when I saw the brightest colors
and everything was mine.
When the pyramids were not the wonders on this earth—
but everything that had been!

Goodbye, Old Town (2006)

Goodbye, old town, at last I'm free!
The house is on the ground; the paint all gone;
the streets driven bare; generations gone.

Goodbye, old town; parents long dead;
the old church testimony to their wake.
Trees that once stood, no longer there.

Goodbye, old town, I only came to see
how in my heart, you never were for me.
I take the road ahead to find the happy me.

Ghosts of My Hometown (2008)

There's nothing left of that little town;
no one to see, no one to call.
The hot dusty alleys behind every house
are now filled with echoes
of long ago children—their dogs and their cats—
of parents calling, *you have school tomorrow,*
come in from your games!

The very cold winters; the church just two blocks;
the guilt of security; the porch in the front;
the voices of grownups like in a dream;
the visits to relatives
and stars were so many,
and summers so long
in that small dreamlike town.

Farewell

"Farewell" is not a favorite word for most of us. Even when parting is necessary, or a suffering person at last gets relief, goodbyes often leave behind them their own trails of conflicting emotion.

But "farewell" can also be celebratory...triumphant...and hopeful.

In this case, we are bidden "farewell" with a smile, a wave, and a kiss. And we are better for the journey.

Don't Weep for Me (1997)

If I should have to go
down that road that we, on our own,
must travel with no one else to guide us,
I know I'll be all right—
for I know I've been there before.

Do not be sad; I know you've been
with me before, and again we'll meet.
And from the place I'll be,
my soul will watch for you.

And when I'm gone, remember only the good,
for your sadness and your pain
would surely keep me from my joy.

Do not be sad or afraid for me,
for I know at last I will have found
my green trees, my fields, my country roads,
at long last home!

Printed in the United States
By Bookmasters